IRELAND'S
OTHER
HISTORY

To Hannah, Coll and Rose with all love,
and in memory of two remarkable women,
Honor Smith and Alice Stewart,
who inspired my youthful quests for knowledge.

IRELAND'S OTHER HISTORY

HECTOR McDONNELL

THE LILLIPUT PRESS
DUBLIN

First published 2012 by
THE LILLIPUT PRESS LTD
62–63 Sitric Road, Arbour Hill,
Dublin 7, Ireland

A CIP record for this title is available from
The British Library.

1 3 5 7 9 10 8 6 4 2

ISBN 978 1 84351 612 5

Typeset by Marsha Swan in 11 on 13pt Dante
Printed and bound in Spain by GraphyCems

Contents

PREFACE

I must beg all readers of this book to proceed with caution. Any journey into the past is a descent into the uncertain, and this attempt to illuminate our origins is only one of a myriad that could be composed. The ancient documents we rely on were all written by fallible people, and for the earliest times we depend upon archaeology, linguistics, DNA analyses, dendrochronology and other specialist fields, all of which raise more questions than answers.

As far as I could, I have tried to show how Ireland's 'otherness' reflects not only its isolation but also how it transformed the influences that reached it. In some instances, as at Newgrange or with the high crosses, they were turned into the most stunning and original creations. Often, too, what seem to be local oddities turn out to be ancient survivals. For example, the rites performed at St Patrick's Purgatory at Lough Derg, Co. Donegal, until the 1630s, must have derived from the Stone Age shamanistic practices used to induce hallucinations that were thought to be contacts with spirit worlds. Equally, the many Iron Age stone heads (the Celts believed that heads of the dead still housed their spirits) had an ancient pedigree. In the earliest Neolithic settlements of the Near East, such as Jericho, skulls were refleshed with clay and plaster, and given cowrie-shell eyes.

We should also always remember to question every attempt to answer the unknown too cleverly. In the words of the historian Daniel Boorstin (1914–2004), 'The greatest obstacle to discovering the shape of the earth, the continents and the oceans was not ignorance but the illusion of knowledge.'

I. *The Age of Stone*

The Age of Stone

Ice Age: the only ice-free areas were in the Irish southwest; no evidence of any human presence although some small animals and reptiles did live here.

c.13000 BC. End of Ice Age.

c.8000–7000 BC. Sea levels rise and Ireland becomes an island.

c.7000 BC. Mesolithic sedentary hunter gatherers settle in Ireland.

c.4300 BC. Neolithic cattle brought to the south coast of Ireland.

c.4100 BC. Neolithic settlement of south coast of Ireland.

c.3900 BC. Farming settlements spread through the north of Ireland.

c.3195 BC. Major volcanic eruption on Iceland. Ireland experiences ten years without summers.

Age of henges and passage graves.

c.2300 BC. Copper mines and workers arrive.

LOCATING IRELAND

High up on the cliffs of Inishmore, the largest of the Aran Islands, a Palaeolithic flint hand axe was found wedged into a crevice. It is the oldest manmade object ever found in Ireland, and beyond these cliffs there is only the vastness of the Atlantic. It was not, however, left here by an awestruck nomad but deposited by an Ice Age glacier.

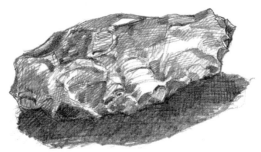

The hand axe from Inishmore, one of only two known Palaeolithic artefacts found in Ireland. Both were probably brought here by glaciers from Britain, where hunter-gatherers lived in ice-free areas during warmer periods of the Ice Age.

Hand axes were the Swiss Army knives of the Old Stone Age. They were developed in Africa more than one and a half million years ago, and were among the tools that enabled *homo sapiens* to spread across the globe. We therefore start our history with an enigma. The Aran axe does not prove that Palaeolithic people ever came here; it may well have been discarded in Britain by one of the hunter-gatherers based there from 40,000 to 18,000 BC during the last warm, 'interstadial period' of the Ice Age, then brought across to Ireland – and battered in the process – by glacial flow.

Parts of southwest Ireland were also ice-free. There is no sign of any human presence – no worked flints, no Irish caves with incised drawings of animals like those in England's Creswell Crags caves, no engraved bones or tusks like those from the Cheddar Gorge. The only other Palaeolithic object ever found in Ireland is a badly worn flint flake from a gravel deposit near Drogheda. A glacier must have brought this one here too, after picking it up en route as it ground its way across Britain and what later became the Irish Sea.

Mesolithic Sites

1. Gobekli Tepe
2. Lepenski Vir
3. Willemstad
4. Tybrind Vig
5. Stonehenge
6. Colonsay
7. Mount Sandel
8. Ferriter's Cove

THE FIRST SETTLERS

*The Irish elk (*Megaloceros giganteus*) went extinct during or shortly after the Ice Age conditions of the Younger Dryas, c.11400–10000 BC. One of the largest deer that ever lived, its range extended from Ireland to Siberia.*

As the Ice Age gave way to warmer conditions around 13,000 BC, hunter-gatherers returned to northern Europe, but they were unsettling times. *Circa* 12,600–300 BC, vast quantities of water melting from the ice sheets in the warming climate poured into the oceans, raising global sea levels by fourteen metres. Then, *c.*10,900 BC, the largest extraterrestrial body to hit the earth in sixty-five million years fell in fragments from Mexico to Syria. Dust clouds filled the upper atmosphere blocking the sun's rays, while the impact's heat caused massive forest fires, melted ice sheets and released vast lakes.[1] Further inundations of meltwater poured into the Atlantic, disrupting the Gulf Stream and raising sea levels again. These ferocious events plunged the northern hemisphere back into Ice Age conditions and several large animal species, including America's sabre-toothed tigers, mastodons and woolly mammoths, went extinct as well as our own greatest native animal, the Irish elk.[2]

This mini Ice Age lasted fifteen hundred years. By 9600 BC, the climate was warming up again and the Gulf Stream returned. Ice sheets shrank, sea levels rose, and by 7000 BC Ireland was an island. This accounts for some of Ireland's best-known 'othernesses', for, ever since, the seas have been both a high road and a moat around Ireland, bringing in boat-loads of people and ideas, but also keeping it apart. Britain, however, was attached to Europe for another thousand years, so snakes, moles and other creatures reached it, creating faunal differences between the two islands that inspired tales about St Patrick ousting undesirable animals from Ireland. Around 1699 Dr Guither, a fellow of Trinity College Dublin, put English frogspawn into a ditch in College Park, and claimed he had reintroduced the common frog (the grass frog, *Rana temporaria*), which the ninth-century St Donatus asserted had been driven out by Patrick.

No savage bear with lawless fury roves,
Nor fiercer lion through her peaceful groves;
No poison there infects, no scaly snake
Creeps through the grass, nor frog annoys the lake.
(Translation by the Revd William Dunkin, 1709–65)

In fact, both men were wrong. Recent research has found the common frog of the Irish southwest to be genetically distinct, and so a species survived there in ice-free locations throughout the Ice Age, in defiance of the national myth.[3]

The frogs of Kerry have a unique DNA signature, indicating that this group survived the Ice Age in an ice-free area, as did several other species including a variety of toad and the Irish hare.

As the ice finally retreated, 'sedentary' hunter-gatherers established themselves in Europe. They had semi-permanent settlements and fish featured heavily in their diet, so these Mesolithic people clustered near rivers and on the coast. Their extensive coastal rubbish heaps, called shell middens, can still be three to five metres tall and over two hundred metres long.

These hunter-gatherers probably reached Ireland in the eighth millennium BC. Antrim's limestone cliffs with their layers of flint were a particular attraction, for flint was the best stone for making tools or weapons with sharp edges, and there are no other flint-bearing rocks in Scotland or Ireland, apart from an outcrop in County Down. The first Irish settlers were therefore particularly active in northeast Ulster, but they also explored the east coast, the Boyne and Liffey river valleys and the Blackwater River in the south.[4]

A Mesolithic harpoon or dagger from the National Museum, Denmark. Sharp flint blades have been fitted into slots in the sides of the deer-bone haft.

These Irish flint flakes represent the typical toolkit of local Mesolithic hunter-gatherers. The smaller blades were fitted into wooden hafts or sockets to make anything from spears to vegetable shredders. The larger flints are from the late-Mesolithic period, when these were preferred over the microliths.

These hunter-gatherers had a versatile range of equipment. Stone axeheads were hafted onto wooden handles, and minute flint blades or microliths were wedged into wood or bone to make spears, arrows, drills and vegetable shredders. Other artefacts also survive, including exquisitely decorated paddles from Denmark, intricate fish traps made from willow branches, nets woven out of willow bast, log boats, bone hooks and harpoons. A tiny wooden effigy from Holland is the sole example of this type.

Supplies were set aside for the leaner times of the year; roots, grains and nuts were stored in pits, and fish or meat dried or smoked. Red meat was in particularly high demand, as one red deer could provide more protein than 50,000 oysters, and even a small group of hunter-gatherers could exhaust a locality's resources. Hazelnuts, for example, were an important food resource, and a group in the Western Isles of Scotland harvested such large quantities on the small island of Colonsay, while also cutting down the hazel trees for fuel, that its woods were gone within a year.

A Mesolithic paddle. Three decorated paddles were found at Tybrind Vig, Denmark, in the 1970s in a settlement site dating from 5500 to 4000 BC and now 3m below sea level. The earliest examples of woven textile were also found here, with thread made from willow bast.

The unique Mesolithic carved wooden figurine from Willemstad in Holland. It was found at 8m below sea level and has a calibrated radiocarbon date of c.5300 BC.

MOUNT SANDEL

Ireland's best-preserved Mesolithic site is at Mount Sandel beside the river Bann, where three or four round huts about six metres across were raised successively in a sheltered hollow. Each hut stood for a season or two. They were made by saplings rammed into the ground, brought together at the top and covered over with skins or brush to provide shelters for about ten people in each. They had hearths in the middle for warmth and cooking, and hut remains nearby suggest others came here too, to hunt, fish and collect plants at particular seasons. They dug pits for food storage and waste disposal, and left behind thousands of used microliths, as well as a few ground stone axes.

The refuse at Mount Sandel contains the bones of young wild pigs killed in winter, of salmon, seabass and flounder caught in the summer, and of eels that came up the Bann in the autumn. The vegetable remains in the storage pits were all late-summer and autumn produce, such as hazelnuts, water-lily seeds and wild apple pips, and the bones of a dozen types of birds were also found. Wood pigeon and mallard predominated, but there were also grouse, snipe, thrush, widgeon, coot, teal, goshawk, red-throated divers, capercaillie and even a pair of eagles. The pigs and birds were probably caught in nets and traps, if not with arrows or spears, while nets, boats, spears, hooks and tackle were used for fishing.

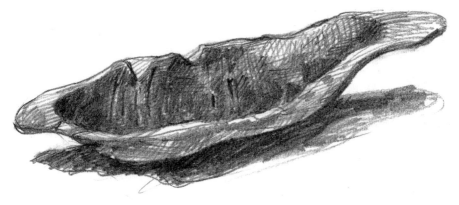

This roughly carved model boat is the only symbolic Mesolithic artefact from Ireland.

Over the centuries the hunter-gatherers explored Ireland's other loughs and rivers as well as the south and west coasts where many worked flints and shell middens are found. A camp site has been excavated at Lough Boora in County

Offaly; at Sruwaddacon Bay in northern Mayo a group gathered hazelnuts; and a dump of burned stone, shell and charcoal beside a well-crafted ground axe at Ferriter's Cove in Kerry looks like the remains of ritual activity. No other possible ritual traces have been identified, apart from a roughly shaped model of a boat, though some Mesolithic flint tools lay under the great Neolithic tombs of the Boyne Valley. In Britain a massive timber alignment of about 8000 BC at Stonehenge indicates that this site was unusually significant thousands of years before the stones were erected, while at Göbekli Tepe in eastern Anatolia an elaborate ritual site arose around 9000 BC. Its tall T-shaped stones weighing several tonnes, and carved with reliefs of many types of creatures, were erected in oval enclosures dug into the ground.

Carvings of a wild boar, fox and scorpion from Göbekli Tepe, eastern Anatolia, dating from c.9000 BC.

No other monuments or artefacts of this quality survive, apart from the half-fish, half-human stone heads of the house shrines of Lepenski Vír in Serbia, a settlement sustained by the huge numbers of fish found near the Danube's Iron Gates. Along with the little effigy from Holland, the Irish model boat and the carvings of Göbekli Tepe, they give us some idea of the imagery of the Mesolithic world.

There were many powers and spirits to appease. Apart from the vagaries of the weather and of fluctuating animal numbers, the sea levels continued to rise dramatically, as ice fields melted, submerging many hunting and fishing grounds,[5] and *c.*6000 BC part of the continental shelf between Iceland and Norway collapsed. This piece was as big as Scotland and unleashed a massive tsunami that swamped low-lying areas around Ireland and Britain, swept far inland and destroyed the land bridge to Europe. The many stories of vast floods and survivors from drowned lands told around the world, Noah and his Ark included, must be folk memories of such inundations. Even the Irish tales about Tír na nÓg, the Land of the Young beyond the Western Sea, may be inspired by traditions about drowned Mesolithic homelands.

Violence was endemic. Ground stone axeheads appear all over Europe, 44 per cent of Danish Mesolithic burials have traumatic injuries to their skulls, and two carefully arranged collections of skulls have been found in Bavaria: men, women and children bludgeoned to death with their heads severed from their bodies. No skeletal remains from the Mesolithic have been found in Ireland, but as well as ground stone axes, large stone clubs are found near the bigger rivers. The later-Mesolithic Irish, as well as those on the Isle of Man, simplified their toolkit, abandoning microliths in favour of larger, simpler flint blades, indicating there was cultural contact between Ireland and at least one of its neighbours.

A carved head on a boulder from a house shrine at Lepenski Vir, a Mesolithic settlement of c.6500 BC in Serbia.

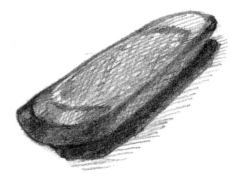

An Irish Mesolithic basalt ground stone axe. These were made by laboriously grinding one stone on another, with water as the lubricant. They appear throughout the Middle East and Europe in the Mesolithic period.

VISIONS AND SHAMANS

These 'entoptic' shapes are hard-wired into human brains to enable the interpretation of visual input. They are frequently seen by people entering a trance state, and are strikingly similar to the images incised onto megalithic monuments.

Hunter-gatherer societies generally believed the world was controlled by spirits, and used shamans as intermediaries. These men thought they could talk to the spirits by going into trances and hallucinating, so they would go through long periods of dancing, drumming or chanting, as well as fasting, sleep deprivation or taking hallucinogenics to induce the right state. Often they went into caves, which were thought to be entry points to spirit worlds. In a trance state, spirals, wavy lines, loops, dots, circles and stars are often seen. These shapes are hard-wired into the brain to help it interpret visual information.

After passing through this state, individuals feel they are moving along a dark tunnel towards a great light. On reaching it, they see things they either fear or want, be they galloping animals, saints, flying creatures, monsters or demons. This is the real hallucination. Generally, shamans described these visions and sometimes turned them into cave art – whether the animals at Lascaux, the bird people of North American Indians or the dancing figures of South African Bushmen.[6]

People often feel they are flying, swimming, changing shape or becoming animals when they are hallucinating, sensations that are vividly expressed in many Irish tales: seals turn into humans, foxes foretell the future and hares leap into spirit worlds. Cú Chulainn went through a hallucinatory transformation that any shaman would recognize:

> The warp-spasm overtook him: it seemed each hair was hammered into his head, so sharply they shot upright. You would swear a fire-speck tipped each hair. He squeezed one eye narrower than the eye of a needle, he opened the other wider than the mouth of a goblet. He bared his jaws to the ear; he peeled back his lips to the eye-teeth till his gullet showed. The hero-halo rose up from the crown of his head.

(From the Táin, translated by Thomas Kinsella)

Inscribed stone from Sess Kilgreen, Co. Tyrone, a richly decorated passage grave on a hill near Omagh, Co. Tyrone.

CAVES AND SPIRITS

Oweynagat in Roscommon, the 'Cats' Cave', has an important place in Irish myth. It lies beneath Connacht's tribal hill, Crúachan, named after Crochain Croidhearg, daughter of the sun goddess Gráinne. One day Crochain fell out of her mother's apron and made the cave her home. Her mother visited her each year at midsummer, when that dawn's light entered the cave. Other spirits came through it at Samhain (the ancestor festival now called Halloween), many of them disguised as cats. They were notoriously dangerous. Bricriu, the Connacht champion, once challenged his Ulster rivals to defeat them. Other spirits emerged from the cave, including small red birds that withered every plant they breathed on, and herds of demonic pigs.

Some myths have extremely ancient roots. The earliest Mesopotamian star charts of *c.*1200 BC describe how the Great Bear constellation's rectangle of stars is the bear, while the three stars protruding from one corner are hunters chasing it across the sky. The same story is told by Siberian hunter-gatherers and North American Indian tribes. As the American Indians' ancestors reached North America *c.*15,000 BC, after which further contact with the Old World was lost, this myth must predate their arrival.

The Egyptian goddess Nut is depicted as a star-studded figure arching across the firmament. She was the goddess of the Milky Way; from her also flowed the Nile.

Another tale depicts the Milky Way as a celestial river flowing from the breasts of a great female who is also the source of an earthly river. This myth developed because the Milky Way touches different points on the horizon at specific seasons and was used to predict the arrival of annual floods. Cultures in Europe, India and China, as well as in North and South America, all have variants of this myth.

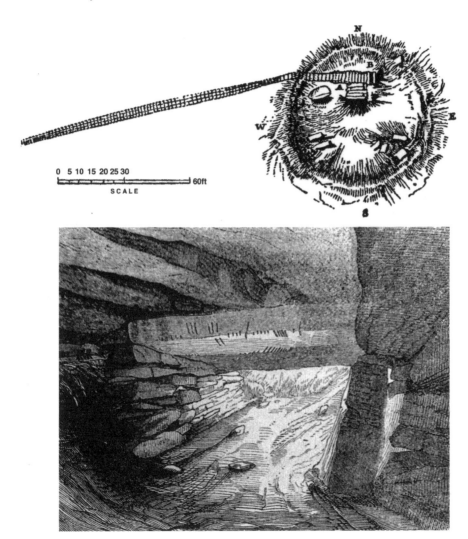

An 1864 print by Samuel Ferguson of the entrance to Oweynagat, the 'Cats' Cave', at Rathcroghan, Co. Roscommon. The ogham inscription reads 'VRAICCI…MAQI MEDVVI': 'of Fraech … son of Medb'. Queen Maedhbh and two men called Fráech feature in epic tales about Rathcroghan, but the ogham stone was only moved here when a souterrain was made c.800–900 AD.

This sky-river spirit image not only appears in dry countries like Egypt where the rains were crucial, but also in Ireland. River floods brought the salmon that were so essential to the hunter-gatherers, and the tale arose that the river Boyne flowed from a spirit being called Bóinn – the wise or white cow – who straddled the sky. Beside the river's source grew Bóinn's alder tree, whose berries contained her powers. Some berries fell into the water where they were swallowed by a salmon that was caught by the young Fionn Mac Cumhaill. He burnt his thumb on the fish while roasting it, and so could conjure up Bóinn's powers at any time simply by sucking on his thumb.

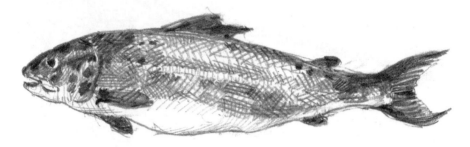

The salmon features frequently in Irish myth. Fionn Mac Cumhaill ate the salmon of knowledge, and as salmon were considered the epitome of health, everyone was said to have a 'salmon of life' inside them.

Similar stories grew up about the Shannon. It was referred to as a *bandéa*, a goddess, and its name comes from Celtic *Senuna*, the 'old honoured one'. Age supposedly brought wisdom and an early Greek writer related that the continental Celts told of a western island ruled by druidesses called *Senae*, 'the old ones'. Another Irish tale told of a woman called Sionainn seeking wisdom from bubbles of knowledge rising from an otherworld, magical well. It overflowed, drowned her, and poured over the land to become the river.

Libraries NI

Derry Central Library
35 Foyle Street
Londonderry
BT48 6AL
Tel 028 71229990

Borrowed Items 06/04/2016 11:25
XXXXXX1424

Item Title	Due Date
The sleeping girl	27/04/2016
Snow White must die	27/04/2016

Thankyou for using this unit

Email
derrycentral.library@librariesni.org.uk
www.librariesni.org.uk

New opening hours to begin from 2nd
November 2015 :
MON, THUR 9am-8pm, TUE, WED, FRI
9am-5.30pm, SAT 10am-4.30pm

AGRICULTURE

This bull was carved on a great standing stone erected at Locmariaquer, Brittany, soon after farming ways arrived in Armorica c.5000 BC. It gives a good impression of the appearance of early-Neolithic cattle.

By the time the Mesolithic hunter-gatherers reached Ireland, the way of life that would supplant theirs had already arisen. Neolithic culture, with its command of agriculture, had developed in the regions of Anatolia around Göbekli Tepe and was now spreading through the Near East. Hunter-gatherers had long harvested wild grains and ground them into flour using saddle querns (the simplest form of grain milling), and sedentary groups in the Near East cultivated gardens for tending edible wild plants. Nevertheless, the invention of agriculture made a dramatic difference. Wild plants yielded to cultivars, their seeds were planted each year in prepared ground; and domesticated breeds of cattle, pigs, sheep and goats evolved.

Farming and herding were a mixed blessing. Although the new ways sustained many more, these people were often malnourished and short-lived, vulnerable to diseases caught from livestock[7] and suffering from arthritis from constant, back-breaking work. The majority of children died in infancy, few men lived beyond thirty-five or women beyond twenty. By contrast, hunter-gatherers typically looked well-nourished and fit, and though adults had a good life expectancy even well-favoured places never supported large numbers. The sedentary

Mesolithic people also had serious problems, for in addition to raising the sea level, the ice-melt waters flooding into the ocean reduced its salinity, which affected the size and vigour of the oyster and mussel beds.

The new farming lifestyle is often described as the 'Neolithic package'. People had to learn how to plant, tend, harvest and process crops successfully as well as maintain domesticated animals and organize villages. Everyone had to learn this lore, which was transmitted orally, through recitation and ritual, as well as taboos and beliefs. The hunting of wild animals also continued, with long bows, slings, nets, throwing sticks and spears, as in earlier times.

The Neolithic package not only brought in pottery but also other cooking tools such as stone mortars and pestles. In the northern parts of Ireland, the pots are heavily influenced by British Neolithic styles. They were round-bottomed, mostly had shoulders two-thirds of the way up their bodies and often had marks of grain on them.

By 7500 BC, Neolithic ways reached the Mediterranean coast. Here they learnt about boats from hunter-gatherer communities and put them to new uses, some settling on Cyprus, others on Crete. Pottery was invented five hundred years later, and was adopted by all farming communities. By 6000 BC, a network of villages covered the islands and coasts of eastern Greece, and, after this, the westward Neolithic expansion split. One part headed north into central Europe, where cattle acquired a new importance as these people became lactose tolerant. Their communities spread out from the Ukraine to northern France, favouring hills with light soils that were cultivated relatively easily with open ground for pasture. Their remarkably uniform culture was known as LBK (Linearbandkeramik) from the distinctive linear decorative bands on its pottery.

By contrast, the southern Neolithic depended upon boats. They gradually colonized the Mediterranean's islands and northern coastlines, bringing grape cultivation and distinctive pottery, and reached southern Iberia in five hundred years.[8] DNA evidence reveals that even when they later reached Ireland, the male Neolithic line was still almost 100 per cent Anatolian while the female line was about 70 per cent indigenous. It must have been standard practice for the young men of established communities to strike out to create new ones, taking most of their women from the local hunter-gatherers. This also ensured that the new settlers acquired local alliances, knowledge and lore.[9]

Log boats were some of the earliest seagoing craft used, mostly for inshore work. This Neolithic example was found below the high waterline at Greyabbey on Strangford Lough, Co. Down.

Neolithic European Spread

In this extremely simplified version of the Neolithic spread, single dates are approximately those of the earliest signs of Neolithic culture in particular areas.

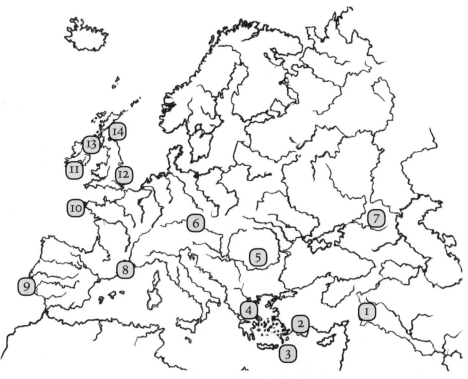

1. Development of Neolithic farming in the eastern Anatolian northwestern Middle Eastern area, 10,200–8800 BC.
2. Farming communities appear along southern Anatolia and Cyprus c.8500–7000 BC.
3. First Cretan settlements, 7000 BC.
4. Development of Neolithic culture on Greek mainland, 6500 BC.
5. Starcevo-Crig copper culture, 6000–3000 BC.
6. LBK culture fl. 5500–1500 BC; spread from Hungary to Holland and northern France.
7. Pontic Steppes herding culture from 6000 BC.
8. Spread of Neolithic settlements along the northern shores of the western

Mediterranean and to the islands, arriving in southern Spain, 5500 BC.
9. Neolithic settlements close to Mesolithic communities on the western Iberian coast, 5000 BC.
10. Settlement of Armorica and Normandy, 5000–4700 BC.
11. Earliest Neolithic contacts on the southern Irish coast, 4500 and 4300 BC.
12. Appearance of Neolithic settlements in East Anglia, 4300 BC.
13. Arrival of LBK culture in northeast Ulster.
14. LBK culture established in southwest Scotland, 3800 BC.

ARMORICAN ARRIVALS AND ULSTER FARMERS

Around 5100 BC, both Neolithic streams reached the western edges of Europe. The Central European LBK version reached inland Normandy and the Low Countries but then took several hundred years to get to the coast, for well-established Mesolithic communities living on maritime resources blocked their way. They lived off the rich maritime environment, resources that had little appeal for the LBK people, as analysis of their teeth shows a total lack of fish in their diet.

Part of the Mediterranean strand, meanwhile, went inland along the river valleys of southern France towards the Atlantic, while other groups kept to the coastlines, passed Gibraltar and founded settlements near the Mesolithic communities on Iberia's western coast. The two groups merged, and an Atlantic Neolithic culture developed whose boats transported people, animals, goods and ideas to new sites along the coast. Much further north, inland Armorica was penetrated from the east by the LBK culture; coastal Mesolithic groups took on cattle, and later the entire 'package' arrived. On the coast, however, the Neolithic culture was heavily influenced by southern French and Iberian traditions, and around 4500 BC it made contact with Ireland.

This first Irish–Neolithic contact is known only from cattle bones and pottery fragments found in places two hundred kilometres apart on the Kerry and Waterford coasts. Pottery was unknown to the Irish Mesolithic culture and

One of the earliest groups of megalithic tombs arose near the north Co. Antrim coast, marking one of the first Neolithic settlements.

hunter-gatherers believed that only shamans could influence animals, so the arrival of people in ocean-going boats with biddable creatures and containers of baked clay would have been impressive, particularly as there were no aurochs (wild cattle) in the country.

For about two more centuries there are no traces of any further contacts. Then, *c.*4300 BC, boats again arrived from Armorica, bringing livestock, seeds, tools, pottery and people. Cattle arrived in Kerry, woods were felled and crops were planted. These colonists also sailed along the Atlantic coastlines, settling on the Sligo and Mayo coasts, in north Antrim, on Scottish Arran and Skye, and in Anglesea and Dyfed in Wales. They built megalithic passage graves of an early Armorican type at these places, and Armorican or Norman versions of 'maritime' LBK pottery were found in several of them.[10]

A new seagoing cultural dynamic was at work. Neolithic communities from Normandy and Flanders crossed the sea to settle in eastern Britain, and their version of the LBK culture reached Wales by *c.*4000 BC. A hundred years later they were in Ulster and by 3800 BC had settlements in the Scottish southwest. In both places farming communities arose in which individual families lived in single houses set amongst fields. This tradition may even have produced Ireland's first Neolithic artwork, a roughly shaped clay figurine supposedly found in a cave in the Antrim limestone cliffs. Flint miners left little shrines or figurines in the tunnels they carved to follow the flint seams, but the authenticity of this one is doubtful.

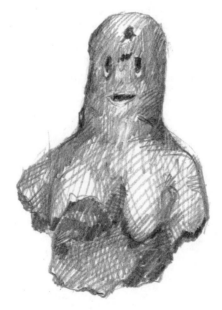

This highly suspect figurine from a flint working on the north Co. Antrim coast is the only possible example of early Neolithic human imagery in Ireland.

NEW BEGINNINGS

Farming communities gradually spread across Ireland. As well as livestock, wheat and barley they cultivated peas, fava beans, lentils, flax and linseed, and tended crab apples.[11] The upper layers of the shell middens reveal the incomers' impact on the Mesolithic Irish, for pottery fragments, Neolithic flint tools, and butchered livestock bones are mixed amongst the later maritime debris. The two communities must have exchanged produce until the sedentary people by the waters' edges dwindled away.

Neolithic pottery provided storage and cooking possibilities unknown to the Mesolithic world. Inevitably, the north-Irish strand of this culture, with its British links, shared many characteristics with the LBK line, and made round-bottomed pots with shoulders two-thirds of the way up, above which they curved inwards or outwards. Over the centuries, new pot shapes and decoration appeared, either representing local changes or the arrival of new traditions or people.

Developing styles of Irish–Neolithic pottery: Carrow-keel ware of the third millennium BC, and a 'Good-land' bowl from Annaghmore, Co. Tyrone.

The north-Irish communities used LBK construction methods, laying down rectangles of timber beams in trenches upon which they built wooden-framed houses. However, houses with rounder plans also appeared, with wooden uprights stuck directly into the ground and sometimes strengthened with low walls. These may have been an indigenous development, but building in the round had been general in the earliest Neolithic phases in the Near East and had spread westwards along the Mediterranean and beyond, though rectangular houses superseded it elsewhere. Very similar roughly rounded buildings were also made in Armorica.

These easily constructed houses fitted into a lifestyle that in the later Neolithic came to rely heavily on transhumance (the seasonal movement of livestock between different pastures). As a result, temporary summer and winter houses were essential. Roundhouses continued to be the norm in Britain until the Romans arrived and in Ireland until Viking times. House shapes and orientations have cultural implications, for as sunlight entered through doorways each day and moved around inside, whole mythologies and traditions were replayed. Particular areas were set aside for specific tasks and rituals at certain times of the day, and also for different social groups and ages.

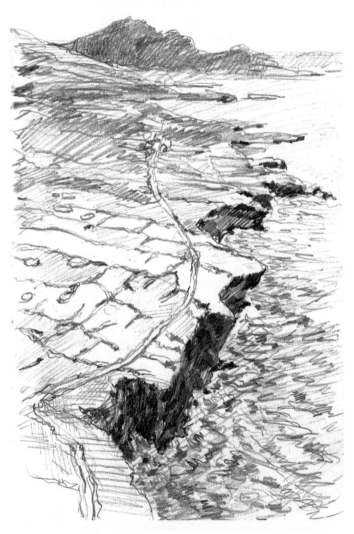

The Céide Fields in Co. Mayo c.3600 BC. The enclosures were for stock management as well as crop planting.

An ard plough could only create a light furrow. Its phallic
shape may be no coincidence.

In some respects, these Irish early-Neolithic settlements created a familiar rural scene: houses sat amongst small fields surrounded by banks and hedges that were used for cattle and agriculture, the ground was turned with spades to make raised beds ('lazy beds') for cereals and vegetables.

The stone head of an ard (a primitive plough) has been found on Island-magee in County Antrim, for yoked pairs of oxen now forced these points into the soil, opening it for the coming season's crops. Some tribal authority must have organized work on large-scale projects such as land clearance, as the networks of fields and ditches required even more labour than megalithic tombs. The best surviving example of this enterprise, the Céide Fields in Mayo of *c.*3700 BC, is the largest early field system in the world.

Orkney voles are genetically most akin to voles in France or Spain but not to their British
counterparts. They are thought to have come to Orkney on Neolithic boats.

Around 3700 BC, large ditched and palisaded enclosures were created on some hills with 'causeways' leading over the ditches. Causewayed enclosures were also made in Britain and neighbouring parts of continental Europe, more for local ritual or assembly than as fortified places. Like the Céide Fields, these relate to increasing tribal power, and similar sites were integral features of Irish life for millennia – assembly places and enclosures where communities shared their produce or assembled fighting forces, settled disputes, elected leaders or held festivities. A few, including the Lammas Fair in Antrim and the Puck Fair in Kerry, survive in modern form.[12]

The Neolithic Irish did not usually construct villages but there is a small one at Ballygally on the Antrim coast built to satisfy the demand for worked flints. Desirable goods moved long distances, so pottery arrived from southern England as well as the Western Isles, and axeheads from Cumbria, Wales and beyond, while Antrim's own axeheads and worked flints spread through Britain. The living proof of this sea traffic is the Orkney vole. It belongs to a European species from either France or Iberia, otherwise absent from the British Isles. The remains of other vole species are found, however, particularly in Irish megalithic tombs, probably because they provided nutrition on long sea voyages and for the soul on its way to the afterlife.

Similarly, recent research reveals that an Irish snail is genetically identical to ones from the eastern Pyrenees where they were an important part of the Mesolithic diet, but different from those of Britain or anywhere else in Western Europe. These snails seem to have been brought to Ireland directly from Iberia by 6000 BC, presumably for their nutritional value, and are therefore evidence of long-distance travel and cultural contacts even before the first Neolithic arrivals.

Neolithic pot from Ballykeel portal tomb, Co. Armagh.

STONE POWER

During the Neolithic period many stone varieties were used to make tools and weapons, but the most versatile of all was flint, which made sharp-edged tools and weapons and sparked fire when struck. Many Neolithic bodies have been found with flint weapons embedded in them and on Islandmagee in County Antrim a scatter of arrowheads was found in a burnt house. They were all burnt by heat, suggesting they were used as fire arrows to set the house ablaze.

Porcellanite, a finely grained volcanic rock, was used for making good-quality polished axeheads. Two seams were mined near the north-Antrim coast – one at the top of Tievebulliagh Mountain, the other on Rathlin Island – and the axes were distributed throughout Ireland and Britain. Fine axeheads were prized since at least the fifth millennium BC and the most sought-after came from a jadeite seam near a peak in the Italian Alps. It was extensively exploited while more easily reached seams were ignored, and one of these jadeite axes even made its way to the Erris Peninsula in Mayo. A large block was also carried from the Alps to northern France to be worked into finished products there, and Britain's best axes came from a greenstone seam near the top of Scafell Pike in Cumbria.

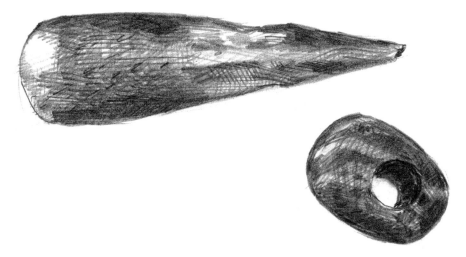

The most prestigious stone items in Neolithic times were highly polished axes and maces, the direct descendants of Mesolithic ground stone axes, and were mostly made from particularly beautiful varieties of stone.

These axeheads travelled large distances through a gift-and-exchange system, and were often kept in large hoards. Many were too large to be practical and as it could take well over a hundred hours to polish one, they became statements of personal importance. They also reveal Neolithic beliefs in the magical properties of beautiful stones from spirit boundaries. The proto-Indo-European **akmon*, the origin of our word 'axe', also yielded words for sky, stone hammers and thunder gods' missiles. It was common rural folklore that stone axes were thunderbolts, and flint arrowheads were elf-shots.[13]

Neolithic arrowhead, Carrowreagh, Co. Down.

MEGALITHS

The creation of Göbekli Tepe c.9000 BC shows that the drive to build elaborate sacred monuments in the Near East predates the Neolithic revolution. It spread with it, and so the LBK communities of northern Europe made longhouses for their dead. These were later encased in earthen mounds, and facades, kerbs and passages made with large stones, initiating the northern megalithic tradition.

Armorica is pivotal to this tradition. Already in Mesolithic times, small stone tombs were made in its shell middens, but the large monuments only arose there after the LBK Neolithic package arrived c.4700 BC. Powerful elites were clearly in control. Vast stone mounds with passages to funerary chambers were built, mainly oriented towards seasonal events such as solstice sunrises and with impressive objects in the tombs, while single standing stones or alignments appeared elsewhere. Bulls, axes, sperm whales and throwing sticks were carved onto some, motifs also used in western Iberia.

Part of the Göbekli Tepe ritual complex, Turkey, of c.9000 BC. After a length of time, ritual settings like this would be dismantled and buried, and a new one built on top of it, a process that continued for hundreds of years.

One of the earliest megalithic tombs at Carrowmore cemetery, Co. Sligo.

The Grand Menhir Brisé, Brittany, is the third-heaviest stone in the world to have been moved and raised with no mechanical aid.

The Grand Menhir Brisé at Locmariaquer, Brittany, the largest stone put up anywhere in Neolithic times, weighed 348 tonnes, stood over twenty metres high and had a sperm whale carved across it. The next stone in this alignment, which possibly pointed at the moon's most southerly setting positions, was fourteen metres high. These stones needed the combined effort of hundreds of people to shift, and dating evidence for any of them is patchy, but the earliest-dated passage graves are from early in the fifth millennium BC both in Armorica and Iberia. West-Iberian artefacts also turn up in Armorican tombs so sea voyages must have brought ideas and objects along the Atlantic Fringe. Armorican-style passage graves appeared on the Irish and west-British coasts *c.*4300 BC, marking the earliest settlements.[14]

The Neolithic settlers of northeast Ulster, by contrast, belonged to the LBK tradition, and their court cairns started as wood and clay houses that were burnt and replaced by stone and earth monuments. Court cairn construction varied. Passage-like stone chambers covered by cairns held in place by kerb stones opened onto stone-lined courtyards where large fires or funeral pyres were lit. At Ballyalton in County Down a monolith marked the court's outer limit, along with an earth bank full of broken pottery and bones, the sweepings of past rituals. A stone from its facade was later taken out and a pit dug and filled with a deposit of forty-four worked flints and a spindle whorl. At another spot, a well-decorated pot sat on a flagstone above a pit of black earth mixed with charcoal, bones, teeth, broken pots and worked flints. There were twenty fine bowls found in this court cairn, along with sheep, dog, cattle and pig bones from many feasts or offerings.[15]

Only about seven people were interred at Ballyalton, which was quite usual, though in some places several dozen were buried in the same court cairn. The communities' requirements varied greatly. Many cremated the bodies, others put disarticulated bones into the cairns, with skulls and bones in separate areas. Specially decorated pottery using peculiar mixtures of clay, quartz and grit was also made for these sites.

The court cairns' chambers and passages are shaped like birth passages and wombs, but a male theme was also at work. Neolithic farmers believed that men, not women, held the life force, and set up their houses and tombs so that the great male spirit, the sun, would penetrate at potent moments. The megalithic monuments of the Atlantic Fringe are also generally placed in the landscape to look out at other important features, such as mountains, the sea, rivers, headlands and islands. They thus memorialized the community's place in the world.

The custom of making passage tombs also spread across northern, eastern and western coastal regions of Ireland, creating a broad overlap with the court cairns. In many places 'cemeteries' of passage tombs arose and another megalithic form, the portal tomb, also appeared. These were free-standing structures, with three or more upright stones supporting a large capstone, and with entrance

Ballymacdermot court cairn, Co. Armagh, a good example of a court cairn. Fires were burnt in the semi-circular court and human remains stored in the long chamber beyond.

looking towards sunrise. They appeared in Iberia and Armorica before spreading to the Cornish, Welsh and Irish coasts *c*.4000–3600 BC, but there are more in Ireland than anywhere else. Many stand in areas where no previous megalithic activity had occurred, so they mark an expansion as well as an elaboration of the culture. The largest, at Brownshill in Carlow, has a capstone weighing about a hundred tonnes.

Yet another burial tradition developed between Dublin and Limerick, an area with few other megalithic monuments. Its box-like polygonal tombs, called Linkardstown cists, of *c*.3600–3200 BC, consist of stone slabs prized from the bedrock slanting in around individual male burials. Small mounds cover them and they usually contain a particular type of decorated pottery.

Proleek portal tomb on the Cooley Peninsula, Co. Louth. It is about 3m high and the capstone weighs about 35 tonnes. The largest Irish capstone for a portal tomb weighs about 100 tonnes.

TEN YEARS WITHOUT SUMMERS

Analysis of bog-oak tree rings has revealed the climatic variations and upheavals that have affected human society from 5000 BC onwards.

The climate improved steadily between 4000 and 3200 BC, bringing the warm summers and cold winters that favoured cereal growing. More land was cleared and the population grew, until in 3195 BC Irish bog-oak tree rings record a severe downturn. Hekla, Iceland's biggest volcano, had erupted. Greenland's ice cores show the highest sulphuric levels ever recorded and so much dust entered the upper atmosphere that the level of sunlight reaching the earth was drastically reduced for ten years. A similar event in 535 AD appears in John of Ephesus's *Historia Ecclesiae*: 'The sun was darkened for eighteen months, shining only for four hours a day; its light just a feeble shadow. Everyone felt it would never recover.'

Just two or three failed harvests would wipe out the reserves of subsistence farmers. Irish and British surveys and pollen analyses reveal that after the 3195 BC eruption, woods grew back over abandoned farmland, cereal crops ceased to be planted, many settlements were abandoned, and large numbers must have died. Volcanic activity on this scale has many consequences. The eight-month-long Icelandic eruption of 1783 not only led to harvest failures but also to thick mists with a high sulphuric acid content over swathes of Europe for months on end. Over 20,000 people died from breathing in these mists in Britain.

SOLAR RITES

The sun had appeared to be dying during this eruption period, and the consequent harvest failures must have caused appalling famines along Europe's Atlantic Fringe. The effects were so severe that it took about four hundred years for the Irish and British communities to recover, a period that has been called the Neolithic Dark Age.[16]

Apart from hunting or catching fish, the survivors must have depended on transhumance, wandering with their livestock between spring, summer and winter pastures. The easily constructed roundhouse was now the norm. The societies that emerged after this collapse were also much more hierarchical. Over the following two centuries, Atlantic Fringe communities devoted enormous amounts of energy to creating vast ritual monuments such as Gavr'inis in Armorica in Brittany, Newgrange and Knowth in Ireland, Stonehenge I and Avebury in England and an elaborate stone complex in Orkney. All are oriented towards significant sunrises, chiefly the solstices.

Incised solar image, Loughcrew, Co. Meath. Sunlight crosses this stone when it enters the tomb at the equinox sunrise.

Powerful elites must have organized this work. Most remarkably, the communities put up ritual monuments from two completely different traditions, as stone circles or circular-banked enclosures called henges as well as passage graves were now made in Ireland and Britain. Enormous pits were also dug, as if to reach into the earth's bowels, but the great focus was the sun, and its extremes of summer strength and winter weakness.

Some of the engraved stones of Gavr'inis passage tomb in Armorica. This monument is probably slightly earlier than the similarly decorated ones in Ireland, such as Newgrange, Co. Meath.

Examples of Grooved Ware like these are found at many Irish and British henges and important passage graves.

The first flat-bottomed pottery appeared in the British Isles, called Grooved Ware from its incised geometrical patterns. It originated in Orkney, where stupendous monuments, stone circles at either end of an enormous temple complex,[17] were also built, before spreading through Britain and Ireland. It is generally found at Irish and British henges and decorated passage graves, and has similar decoration. The larger vessels were probably meant for beer or mead, the earliest organized alcohol production in northern Europe. Chemical analysis

Carved stones in Locmariaquer tomb in Brittany.

The entrance of Newgrange, Co. Meath, with its blocking stone in place.

of pots from Fife reveals that these also held black henbane (*Hyoscyamus niger*), a powerful hallucinogen, suggesting that drinks concocted in these vessels were intended for inducing hallucinatory experiences. Similarly, polypods, small shallow bowls with feet, including one found at Newgrange, held small quantities of substances that were probably burnt for their hallucinogenic effects.[18]

Although Grooved Ware originated in Orkney and is contemporary with the temple complex, the impetus for creating large, well-oriented passage tombs came from the south. The highly decorated passage grave of Gavr'inis in Armorica has a calibrated radiocarbon date of 330–3100 BC, which puts the 3195 event in the middle of its range. Its intensely organized carvings closely relate to those of Newgrange and both tombs point to mid-winter sunrise. At Newgrange the sun enters on that day through its roof box, a window-like opening above its entrance.

Another passage grave four kilometres from Gavr'inis at Locmariaquer points at midsummer sunrise. The capstones of both tombs are broken sections of a fourteen-metre-high standing stone, which had a sperm whale, an axe and a bull carved on it, while another reused stone at Locmariaquer sports crooks or throwing sticks. There are many carvings and stone models of these boomerang-like throwing sticks in Armorica and Iberia, so they were clearly significant objects. Tutankhamen is also depicted in a tomb painting using a throwing stick to hunt duck and although no Irish examples survive, there is a Neolithic throwing stick from Ehenside Tarn in Cumbria.[19]

Presumably, the Gavr'inis builders' ideas reached Ireland, as very similar designs are used in the Bend of the Boyne and Fourknocks tombs, which also show Iberian influences. It is suspected that the large Irish passage graves were built for the elites of over twenty separate territories covering much of the northern and eastern parts of the country. These monumental graves often stand on hills within sight of their neighbours, some in cemeteries of older tombs, and often with vast stone cairns raised on nearby hills, as in Sligo and at Loughcrew. (Silbury Hill near Avebury is the largest of these artificial hills, and there are several in Armorica.)

Stone from a passage grave at Loughcrew,
Co. Meath, incised with entoptic patterns.

The cemeteries incorporate varied traditions, and several had already existed for over a thousand years. Some smaller passage graves point towards major tombs and others at significant local landmarks. The large passage-grave orientations are equally varied. At Loughcrew one faces the equinox sunrise while the other faces the Samhain dawn, the festival now known as Halloween. (This alignment also gives 'Imbolc' on the other side of the winter solstice, the start of pagan Irish spring on the first of February, now St Brigid's Day.)

The patterns on the north stone at Newgrange, Co. Meath, differ from those on the entrance stone, but both centre on lines indicating the direction of the passage inside the mound, and use diamond and spiral patterns.

Other cosmic events were also targeted. Knowth's passages are aimed at equinox sunrises and sunsets, others are oriented towards extreme positions of the moon's 18.5 year cycle and Baltinglass tomb in the Wicklow Mountains looks at the pole star, while the Sligo cemeteries' passage tombs point at the enormous cairns on nearby hills. One of these was said to house the warrior goddess Maedhbh and, intriguingly, the great Andalusian tomb of Cueva de Menga was oriented at a mountain containing an elaborately painted cave.[20]

Basin and remains of passage tomb on the summit of Baltinglass Hill in the Wicklow Mountains.

The objects buried in the great Irish passage tombs are those of rich elites. In some places, all the burial deposits were put in soon after the tombs were built, while others were used for long periods. At Knowth, the ashes of about two hundred people were deposited over a period of three hundred years.

The three great tombs of the Boyne are radiocarbon-dated to *c.*3200–3000 BC, that is, to the period after Hekla's eruption, and 80 per cent of all the megalithic art of Europe is engraved on them. Smaller passage tombs, henges and cursuses were all packed together around them, indicating extensive and complex usage over a long period.

Just across the Irish Sea from the Boyne are two decorated passage tombs on Anglesea. They use the same construction methods and have similar incised patterns to the Boyne tombs. The only other British example, at Calderstones near Liverpool, has foot outlines as well as spirals on its stones. No human features appear on Irish megalithic carvings, although they do in Armorica. The passage-grave tradition also spread through the Scottish Isles and Scottish east coast, from where it went on to Orkney and southern Scandinavia. There were clearly close contacts with Ireland, for about fifty Irish-looking passage graves are found between Inverness and Aberdeen and a further eighty in Orkney. Maes Howe, the most impressive, of *c.* 2800 BC, was oriented towards the winter solstice sunset and like Newgrange had a 'roof-box' arrangement to let in the sun after the entrance was blocked. Another Orkney tomb has the same roof-box system, and stones with incised spirals like those on the Boyne tombs are found on another.

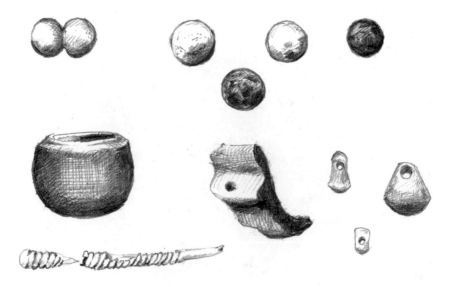

Some of the finds from Newgrange, Co. Meath. Similar drilled pendants are found in many graves and the double ball shown here could be a toggle; the purpose of the single balls, however, is unknown. Bone pins are found in many burials, some being up to a metre long.

Most curiously, the Maltese megalithic culture also seems to have some influence. They developed the technique of rolling heavy stones on stone balls running along grooves in long planks, *c.*3500 BC, and word of this 'ball bearing' technique must have reached the Atlantic Fringe as it was also used at many British megalithic sites and probably in Ireland, as well. The Maltese temples also have solar orientations.

Finely carved and polished penis-shaped object from Knowth, Co. Meath.

This macehead from Knowth, Co. Meath, is one of the finest carved and polished flints known.

SPELLS

The culture that developed after the Hekla eruption seems to have been a sun-oriented theocracy, and vestiges of these beliefs are found in early legends. Several Irish mythical figures began as sky deities, and Irish royal lineages often traced their descent from them. The quartz used on the tombs was believed to hold the sun's rays or its semen, a belief enhanced by the electrical discharges caused when two pieces were struck together. Quartz was used at many megalithic sites on the Atlantic Fringe, including Gav'rinis,[21] and I suspect that the elite buried in the tombs claimed they had a personal relationship with the sun. Presumably they thought this would protect them against future disasters but to no avail, for the sun's near death in 3195 BC was only the first of many similar cataclysms.

The rites and rituals performed at the Irish megalithic sites have left few traces, but by Knowth's two entrances there are cobbled, basin-like depressions and a number of cobbled semi-circles set against the kerbstones, while Newgrange had one large, cobbled oval near its entrance. These cobbles are mostly 'exotics' like quartz, granite and banded mudstone that were probably felt to have magical associations, while many small quartz pieces lay on the cobbles. One suggestion is that the depressions were filled with water on particular occasions and the quartz pieces thrown into them, creating circular ripples like the designs on the stones. Some unusual objects come from these cobbled settings, including pestle-like stones with simple carved decoration and stones shaped like penises. One, with undulating ribs and a groove running its length, is similar to some from southwestern Iberia. Well-shaped stone lamps were also found and a fragment of a polished stone bowl as fine as those of Crete or Egypt.[22]

Many megalithic tombs contained quantities of mussel and oyster shells, mostly unopened. As Neolithic people generally avoided eating fish, these molluscs probably had a magical purpose. Shellfish are found in Neolithic tombs all over the Atlantic Fringe, and even two thousand years earlier on Cyprus. Clam-shell necklaces were common and personal ornaments made from spondylus shells from the Aegean were popular with Neolithic communities all the way from Greece to Normandy. Most intriguingly, a ring from a sperm-whale tooth was found in a Carrowmore tomb in Sligo, for Armorican and Iberian carvings show that sperm whales were highly revered.

The greatest insight into the magic invoked at these sites comes from the Anglesea decorated passage tombs. On the floor of Barclodiad y Gawres were the remains of a magical brew of the mid-third millennium BC: a concoction of eel, whiting, wrasse, frog, toad, snake, mouse, shrew and rabbit. The brew had been poured over a fire burning in a cobbled circular hearth similar to the cobbled settings at Knowth and Newgrange, and then covered over with earth mixed with quartz, rounded pebbles and shells.

The other Anglesea tomb, Bryn Celli Ddu, a late-Neolithic construction, made a forceful statement about cultural change, as it is built over a demolished henge monument. Before its entrance were human and cattle bones; a fossilized tree trunk stands in its chamber as if growing there, and behind the chamber's back wall was a standing stone covered in incised designs from the old henge. It was lying down over a fire pit whose ashes contained a human ear bone.

An ivory bracelet from a Carrowmore tomb, Co. Sligo. It was made either from a sperm-whale tooth or a walrus tusk. These were considered animals with great magical powers, for they crossed spirit boundaries as they breathed air on the surface and then dived into the sea's depths.

The unusually heavily decorated bowl from Knowth's eastern passage, Co. Meath.

The great tomb at Knowth was also built over an older ritual site. Its satellite tombs predate it but are aligned towards the mound as if there was already something important there, and several of the decorated stones seem to be reused. Below the mound were early-Neolithic rectangular houses and later roundhouses, and an unusual, elaborately carved stone bowl stands in a niche at the end of its east passage. It must have been there before the tomb was constructed as it is too big to have been brought in afterwards and two upright stones further narrow the niche's entrance. A similarly decorated second bowl lay buried in a stone-lined box nearby.[23]

At the entrance to the niche, archaeologists found a superbly carved flint macehead in a burial deposit. Below it were six more burials accompanied by stone beads, pendants and large, ornamented bone pins, remnants of this elite's finery. Another sign of magic at work is that some stones at Knowth and Newgrange have their most decorated sides facing into the mound. Was this done for the spirit world? Some of the larger stones were dragged over twenty kilometres, the granite cobbles came from the Mourne Mountains and tonnes of quartz from the Wicklow Mountains thirty-four kilometres to the south. All of this required organization and control of manpower. Tonnes of quartz were also used for tombs in Westmeath, Sligo, Armagh and Antrim, and each one took years of planning.

A decorated stone from the passage tomb on Knockmany Hill near Augher, Co. Tyrone.

CHAMBERS AND FEASTING HALLS

The large passage tombs were idealized versions of the caves that had been part of shamanistic practices since Palaeolithic times, and were decorated with the patterns seen by those entering a trance state. They also reflected their ideas of how the world was run. At Newgrange, the sky-river goddess Bóinn is held in her house (this is the meaning of its proper name, Brú na Bóinne), waiting for the sun to impregnate her at the end of the year's longest night. For this male-dominated farming society, females were breeding stock and Old Irish *brú* meant a womb as well as a house.

Another peculiarity of Newgrange was that the roof box was closed by blocks of quartz. The sun therefore only entered when these were pulled out, perhaps during midwinter rituals after somebody's ashes had been placed in the tomb, or as part of a yearly ceremony.[24] The triple spiral on the entrance stone mimics that in the back niche of the inner chamber, which the sun lit at the climax of its penetration: was this the goddess's vulva?[25]

The interior of Newgrange, Co. Meath, from the central niche. The triple spiral would have been lit by the sun at the height of its penetration at dawn on the shortest day of the year.

Megalithic Europe Passage Tombs

1. Passage tombs of Andalucia, 3700 BC.
2. Western-Iberian megalithic tombs.
3. Megalithic tombs concentrated along the coastlines of Armorica, *c.*3300–3100 BC.
4. Irish passage graves, mainly concentrated in a belt going from Wicklow to Meath and across to Sligo, as well as a scatter further north, *c.*3200–300 BC.

5. Three British passage tombs from Anglesea to near Liverpool.
6. Orkney.
7. South-Scandinavian passage tombs.
8. North-German passage tombs.

SPIRITS AND LEGENDS

Irish myths describe passage graves, hills and mountains as otherworld dwellings or feasting halls, though often with a Christian veneer. On Slieve Donard, the highest of the Mourne Mountains, there is a megalithic tomb called Donard's Chapel: he was one of the Seven Watchers of Ireland whom St Patrick put inside certain mountains to protect the country until the Second Coming. People could even visit Donard inside his mountain by entering the 'chapel' at certain times.

The passage tomb on Slieve Gullion, the highest peak in Armagh, is the house of Cailleach Bhéarra, the harvest goddess. She changes from hag to young girl to entice men into her depths, and once lured Fionn Mac Cumhaill, who returned an old and broken man. The vast cairn on Knocknarea Mountain above Carrowmore cemetery in Sligo contains the goddess Maedhbh in a chamber, spear in hand, her warriors around her waiting to attack the men of Ulster. Originally she was the earth mother who empowered new rulers; the newly chosen king at Tara had to go through a ritual marriage to Maedhbh and become intoxicated by her (her name is synonymous with mead). 'Great was the power and influence of Maedhbh over the men of Ireland. She permitted no king on Tara until he had her for his wife.' Irish pre-Christian kings were regarded as semi-divine beings who ensured their tribes' success and their lands' fertility through their relationships with an earth goddess and the spirit world.[26]

A crow. Birds feature in Irish mythology as intermediaries with spirit realms. Crows flying round a house are still regarded as harbingers of death.

Several other Irish tribes had Maedhbh as their goddess,[27] so she also lives in a cairn on Knockma in Galway, and in Keshcorran cave below Carrowkeel cemetery in Sligo. Keshcorran was a particularly potent portal to the spirit world, and Maedhbh would change shape, into a greyhound that outran other creatures or a sharp-beaked crow that warned warriors of their coming death.

The legends about Slaghtaverty Giant's Grave, Co. Derry, were related to Bram Stoker, who drew upon them for his great horror story, Dracula.

Macha, the Ulster land goddess, lived inside Emhain Macha, the royal assembly hill near Armagh. She controlled the weather, sent down fogs, storms, blood and fire, and was also a horse goddess. Out of this grew the tale that her husband forced her to race, while heavily pregnant, against the king of Ulster's horses. She won, but died giving birth to twins, and cursed the men of Ulster to suffer birth pangs for nine half-days whenever they went to fight.

Brighid, the mistress of nature, is everywhere too, though her wells, streams, trees and stones now belong to her Christian namesake. On Oímelg, St Brigid's Day on the first of February, she lets ewes' milk flow, and crosses of green rushes, the plant of rebirth, are hung up to ensure her protection.

Patrick Weston Joyce relates a curious legend about a megalithic site in his *Origin and History of Irish Names of Places* (1875).

> There is a place in the parish of Errigal in Derry called Slaghtaverty, but it ought to have been called Laghtaverty, the laght or sepulchral monument of the Abhartach or dwarf. This dwarf was a magician, and a dreadful tyrant, and

after having perpetrated great cruelties on the people he was at last vanquished and slain by a neighbouring chieftain; some say by Fionn Mac Cumhail. He was buried in a standing posture, but the very next day he appeared in his old haunts, more cruel and vigorous than ever. And the chief slew him a second time and buried him as before, but again he escaped from the grave, and spread terror through the whole country. The chief then consulted a druid, and according to his directions he slew the dwarf a third time, and buried him in the same place with his head downwards, which subdued his magical power, so that he never again appeared on earth. The laght raised over the dwarf is still there, and you may hear the legend with much detail from the natives of the place, one of whom told it to me.

When the Abhartach rose from the grave he drank his subjects' blood and the druids declared him to be one of the *neamh-mairbh*, the 'walking dead', who could only die if a yew-wood sword were driven through his body. Joyce was a friend of Bram Stoker at Trinity College Dublin, and this tale inspired him. The druids described the Abhartach as *drochfhola*, 'of bad blood', so Stoker's villain became *Dracula*.

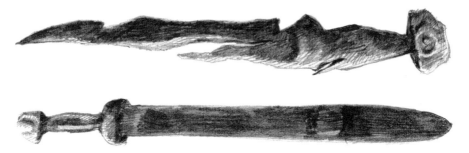

Two Irish Bronze Age wooden swords. The complete one is from Ballykilmurray, Co. Wicklow. Both were found in the nineteenth century in prehistoric graves; the legends collected by Patrick Weston Joyce about Slaghtaverty included one in which the Abhartach's unquiet body was pierced with a wooden sword.

RITUAL CIRCLES

The stone circle at Ballynoe, near the Co. Down coast, was excavated in 1937–8. It was used from the late Neolithic into the early Bronze Age and altered many times. An earth-covered cairn on its east side covered a round stone setting similar to those at Knowth and Newgrange, Co. Meath, while on the west side an oval of cobbles supported a raised platform.

The circular ritual enclosures with solar orientations that appeared in Ireland and Britain at the end of the fourth millennium BC had a long history. Goseck, the earliest-known example, was created nearly two thousand years earlier, c.4900 BC, near Leipzig in Germany, just a few hundred years after the first Neolithic communities developed there. It consisted of three concentric ditches and wooden palisades with openings to let in the sunrises and sunsets of the summer solstice.

There are about 250 circular enclosures of the Goseck type in central Europe. They continued to be made into the Bronze Age, and two thousand years after Goseck three hundred henges with similar orientations appeared in Britain, Ireland and northwest France. Exactly how these traditions relate to one another is a mystery, but the 3195 BC event played a role, as the earliest calibrated radiocarbon date for an Irish henge, Raffin in Meath, is 3100 BC, and Britain's first henges have a similar date.

Often the Irish henges are near major megalithic monuments, and consist of circular earth and stone banks, and ditches with openings towards major solar events. The Bend of the Boyne complex, the Loughcrew hills and the Sligo cemeteries all have henges too but, unlike the passage tombs, henges appear all over Ireland, so they had a much wider appeal.

The Grange circle, Co. Limerick (otherwise the Lios henge: the Irish name is Lios na Gréine, rath of the sun), *is 35m in diameter, dating from the early Bronze Age. It was marked out with the help of a rope tied to a peg at its centre, twelve large orthostats were placed at intervals around the periphery, the largest weighing 40 tonnes, and smaller stones were then fitted between them.*

Some henges, including Tara's, encircled old megalithic tombs. Nearby Ballybattin's massive henge complex was flattened in the eighteenth century, but the Lios near Lough Gur in County Limerick still exists. Its stone-lined bank enclosed a levelled interior and has openings looking at the sunsets of Imbolc and Samhain in February and November as well as at the summer-solstice sunrise. The interior was packed level with clay, and the surface strewn with broken Beaker pottery.

The largest henge of all, the Giant's Ring at Ballynahatty, was created about 2500 BC on high ground above a bend of the river Lagan near Belfast, the only Irish henge complex to be so thoroughly investigated. Its earth embankments are four metres high, and enclose a small megalithic passage tomb. The Ring was originally part of a much larger complex built in the middle of a megalithic cemetery. A wooden henge stood outside the Ring, with a further wooden circular structure inside it that enclosed a square chamber. Between the henge and the Ring's entrance was yet another square wooden chamber containing butchered animal bones and broken pottery. It also had cremation pits on either side.

After about a hundred and fifty years, the complex's decaying timbers were dug up and burnt, after which their ashes were poured back into the empty post holes and covered over with turves. As with the structures in and around Stonehenge and Orkney's Ness of Brodgar, the Giant's Ring group had areas probably set aside for the different stages of a dead person's journey from the world of the living to the realm of the dead. One archaeologist has imagined the rites that may have happened here: a group would carry the body up the hill to an 'ominous wooden facade with a narrow entrance', inside which they would come to a square chamber, where there was feasting and various rituals. After this they took the body through the wooden henge, and either left it to rot at one site and/or to be dismembered or cremated at another. Beyond this was the way into the Ring, and the bleached bones of the ancestors.[28]

There are many Irish stone circles, the megalithic version of the henge tradition. Those on the east coast and in the Sperrin Mountains resemble the early stone circles of Cumbria and must therefore relate to Irish Sea–northwest British maritime connections. Some were built around old tombs, others had new burials placed inside them, and many were littered with the debris of feasts, sacrifices and cremations. Some had levelled interiors, others were filled with stones, some are aligned with astronomical events, others not, some were left alone once they were built and others were rebuilt and used many times.

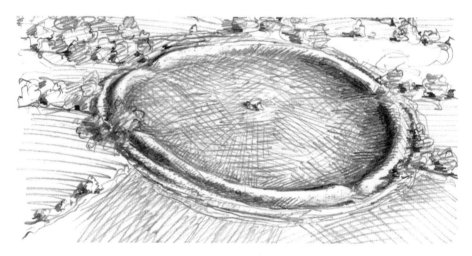

The Giant's Ring, Ballynahatty, Belfast, is 180m in diameter, making it the largest henge in Ireland.

II. *The Age of Bronze*

The Age of Bronze

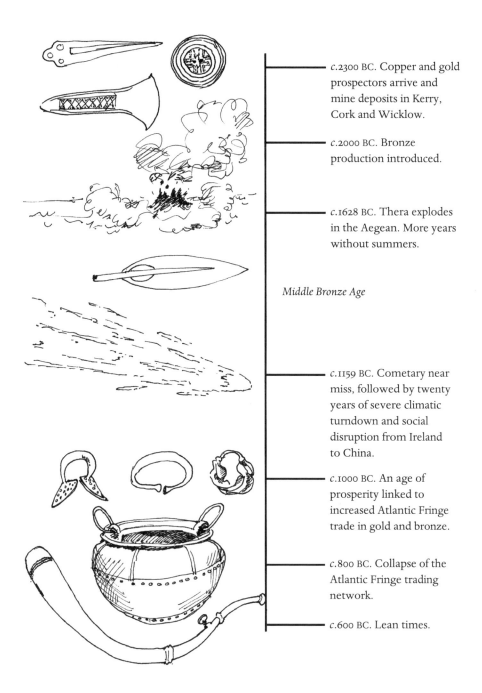

*c.*2300 BC. Copper and gold prospectors arrive and mine deposits in Kerry, Cork and Wicklow.

*c.*2000 BC. Bronze production introduced.

*c.*1628 BC. Thera explodes in the Aegean. More years without summers.

Middle Bronze Age

*c.*1159 BC. Cometary near miss, followed by twenty years of severe climatic turndown and social disruption from Ireland to China.

*c.*1000 BC. An age of prosperity linked to increased Atlantic Fringe trade in gold and bronze.

*c.*800 BC. Collapse of the Atlantic Fringe trading network.

*c.*600 BC. Lean times.

SEA CHANGES

After several hundred years Ireland's population recovered. Agricultural production revived, more henges and passage graves were built, and *c.*2500 BC copper and gold prospectors from Armorica arrived on the southwest coast. They found copper ore in the cliffs' rocks, cut down woods for charcoal, dug mines, and broke open the seams. They made kilns, crucibles and moulds, melted the copper ore and made ingots, weapons and tools.

They were also looking for gold. An appreciable amount existed in Ireland, in alluvial deposits. Nuggets occasionally turn up, but mostly panning is required,

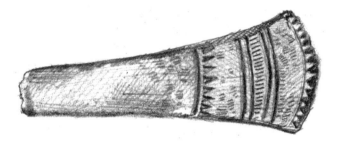

Copper axes were some of the first metal objects made in Ireland.

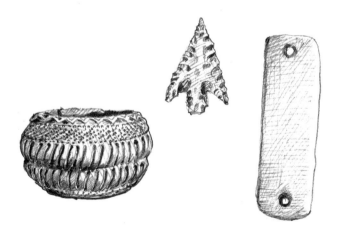

This small pot from Newtonstewart, Co. Tyrone, is one of the earliest examples of Beaker pottery found in Ireland.

Western Europe: Copper, tin and gold mining

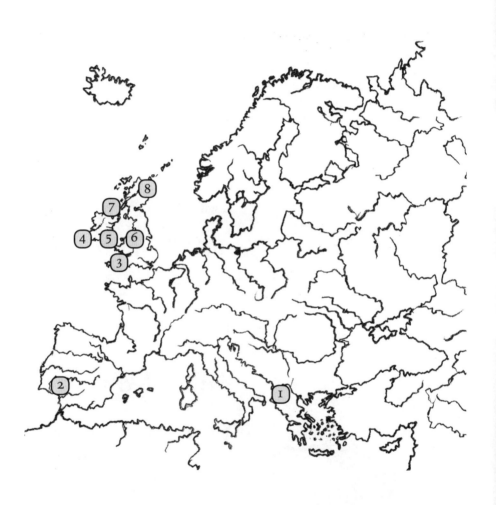

1. Albania	5. Wicklow
2. Tartessos	6. Great Orme
3. Cornwall	7. Corrstown
4. Kerry	8. Inverness

or running the water across sheep fleeces to catch the smallest flakes (hence the Golden Fleece). The last serious effort to extract Irish gold was in the late 1790s, when a mining company working near the Wicklow Mountains extracted 944 ounces of gold in three years, which is about seventy ounces more than the weight of all the extant prehistoric Irish gold.

The early-Irish metalworkers belonged to the Maritime Bell Beaker Culture. A gold- and copper-rich society had flourished for the previous three thousand years in the lower Danube basin (covering much of present-day Bulgaria and Romania), but as it declined its metalworkers moved first to the Adriatic coast around Albania, where there were rich copper seams, then Italy, and finally to southern Iberia. There they met the central European Beaker Culture that had brought into western Europe many of the cultural innovations of the herding societies of the Pontic Steppes. As well as herds of cattle, these people had bred the first wool-bearing sheep, domesticated the horse, had wagons pulled by oxen and devoloped a highly mobile, warrior-led society.[29]

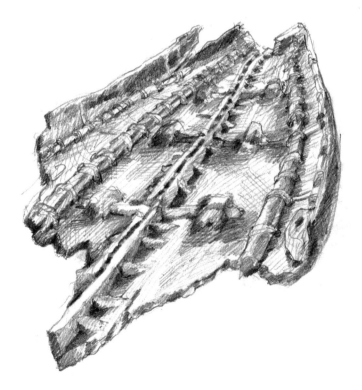

Bronze Age boat found at Dover dating from c.1575–1520 BC. The oak planks were stitched together with yew withies and calked with moss. Its broad beam indicates that it could carry a substantial cargo. Three more similarly built boats of c.2000–1680 BC were found near Ferriby in Yorkshire.

The Maritime Beaker Culture prospered in southern Iberia. It built fortified towns, the first in western Europe, and spread along the Atlantic Fringe with its miners and prospectors. Their craft included a sixteen-metre-long 'stitched plank' boat, a freight-carrying vessel found at Dover. Moreover, their decorated beakers were prestige objects and some were tiny – designed, perhaps, for small measures of potent drinks. Lavish feasting demonstrated a chieftain's power, and strong alcoholic drinks were a further mark of prosperity, for they required effort and ingenuity to produce in northern Europe, where sugar sources were scarce.

In Ireland, different types of Beaker pottery appeared, some from the Atlantic Fringe tradition, others from Britain and Europe. The affluent Irish dead were often buried with one small vessel and a large one too, perhaps for food and drink on their journey to the afterlife, whereas Europeans often took big ewers with them along with a dozen or more cups, as if expecting company.

This Beaker pot of a type known as a Food Vessel was found at Agnahily, Co. Laois. They were commonly placed in single graves.

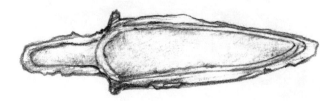

Copper dagger from Galway.

Even small copper items were so highly prized that a knife, axe or awl gave its owner status. Personal property thus became increasingly significant, which led to individual burials: stone-lined cists in which the body lay in a foetal position with perhaps one or two pots, a stone axe, a copper object, archery equipment and gold, or jet or amber fineries. Some of their necklaces were enormous. Amber and jet had been worn since Mesolithic times for their magical properties as they floated on salt water and amber, when rubbed, created an electrical charge. The wearer's status was denoted by their possession and they were presumably held to be imbued with protective or healing powers, as they were in much later times.[30]

One of a pair of gold disks from Tydavnet, Co. Monaghan, the largest and best decorated of all Irish examples. Usually found in pairs, it has been suggested that they might represent either the sun or breasts, and were either hair ornaments or sewn in pairs onto the clothing of significant individuals. They might even relate to the Iron Age custom described by St Patrick of kissing a superior man's nipples.

This burial custom reached Ireland with the Armorican metal prospectors. Irish gold was hard to find, so the earliest objects were thin. Some were pairs of disks hammered with repoussé designs, pierced near the centre by two little button-like holes. The concept came from Armorica, and they were also made in Wales, Scotland, the Isle of Man and Denmark as part of the northward flow of ideas and goods. In return the Irish got amber, jet and horses. The latter were first domesticated by tribal herdsmen on the Pontic Steppes over a thousand years earlier, and gradually spread across Europe. A scatter of butchered bones in Ireland suggests that horses were eaten at the end of their working lives. They were probably used as pack animals rather than for riding, as there are no bit marks on their teeth but the Pontic herdsmen's wool-bearing sheep did not reach here. Irish sheep continued to be of the older 'Soay' variety whose wool was plucked rather than shorn.[31] Even so, the gold disks ornamented clothing perhaps as symbols of the sun and moon.

Buttons like these, made of jet from Whitby in Yorkshire, are found in graves all over Ireland and demonstrate the effectiveness of the Bronze Age gift-and-exchange network. It brought sought-after items over long distances for the benefit of powerful elites.

There were also crescent-moon gold collars called lunulae; two disks and a lunula were found together in 1945 in Coggalbeg bog, near Strokestown, County Roscommon. They are also found in Armorica, Portugal and on Italian rock carvings, so the idea probably came from the Mediterranean to the Atlantic Fringe. Three lunulae were found in a box at Kerivoa in Armorica with some sheet gold and a gold rod with similar flat terminals. All the Kerivoa gold plus another Armorican lunula and one from Harlyn Bay in Cornwall were decorated with the same tool, presumably by the same craftsman. Like the disks, Irish lunulae made their way by gift or exchange to Britain, Normandy and Germany, where they are found in wealthy burials. Eighty have been found in Ireland (only about twenty are known outside Ireland), all of them left as votive offerings in bogs, lakes and rivers. They must have been often in long use. Some were repeatedly rolled up, and one had its original decoration beaten out and replaced.

Open moulds for casting copper objects turn up all over Ireland. Copper smiths must have travelled with ingots, carving moulds as required, but when cooled after smelting, copper weapons remain very soft so they were mainly designed for striking or stabbing. Beautifully decorated axes were prized, as were 'halberds', knife-like blades fastened onto staves at right angles to the hafts to make excellent stabbing weapons. Like the gold lunulae, there were halberds in Italy, Iberia and Armorica, but also in northern Europe. As only those left as votive offerings survive, most are in mint condition, including seven that were grouped together at the bottom of a Galway bog, with their blades pointing down into the earth. In Ireland such offerings were generally left in rivers, bogs and lakes, which were spirit or tribal boundaries.

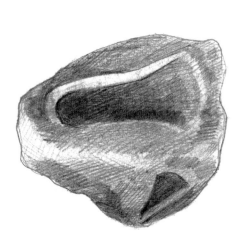

Copper moulds like this one are found all over Ireland. Presumably they were made on the spot by the itinerant smiths who carried copper ingots all over Ireland.

Gold lunula from Ross, Co. Westmeath. Precious objects were usually deposited as votive offerings at tribal boundaries.

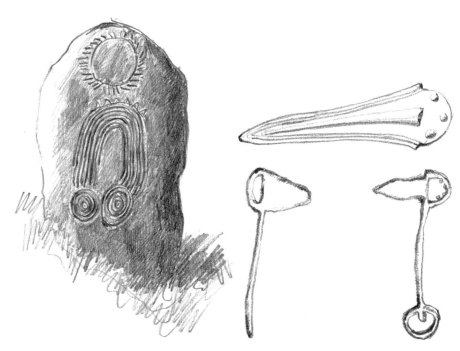

An engraved lunula effigy from Valcamonica, Italy. It is virtually identical to the Irish examples.

Engravings of halberds with wooden handles from Valcamonica in Italy.

BEAKER UPSETS

About a hundred years after the Maritime Beaker prospectors reached Ireland, another major volcanic eruption occurred in 2345 BC, followed by ten more years of misery. The pollen record shows that crop cultivation ceased and grass, weeds and trees grew over abandoned farmland again.

This catastrophe shook Atlantic society. In Orkney the great temple complex was demolished and replaced by an even larger building that was used for one last enormous animal slaughter and feast. No more passage tombs were made in Ireland, but it did not end the old beliefs. More henges and stone circles were built, and burials continued in the old megalithic tombs' mounds for another thousand years, including a hundred or so at Tara's passage grave. Another Armorican group landed in southwestern Ireland, bringing further changes including a new type of megalithic tomb called a gallery grave. The Irish version is known as a wedge cairn and these faced the extreme southwestern setting positions of the moon or sun.

Wedge tomb, Ballybriest, Co. Derry.

Like the earlier megalithic sites, the wedge cairns were for an elite. Only a few were ever interred in them, after cremation on large, labour-intensive pyres. Wedge cairns became popular: there are over five hundred, many in southern and western areas with few previous megalithic tombs. Small stone circles also arose in southwest Ireland. These were inspired by similar traditions to the wedge cairns, for each has a 'recumbent' stone on the circle's southwest side, orienting it towards setting positions of the moon or the sun.

Beaker Culture also introduced composite bows to Ireland. Much shorter than the long bows, these could be carried and fired from horseback. Flint arrowheads and stone wrist guards now appear in graves all over the country, though mostly in the north. Good marksmanship, particularly by a rider, requires constant practice and fine equipment, so their possession was a mark of social importance.

Recumbent stone circle, Drombeg, Co. Cork, one of many erected in the early Bronze Age in southwest Ireland.

Red deer also appeared for the first time in Ireland. To import a breeding herd, deer had to be caught, tethered and brought over in boats, so their arrival would have been a great event. They were a dependable food source even in climatic downturns, as well as suitable quarry for a hunting elite, and butchered bones as well as antler or deer-bone ornaments became usual.

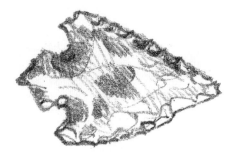

Bronze Age arrowhead from Carnlough, Co. Antrim. It is only 3cm long and must have been designed for hunting small birds or fishing.

CURSUSES AND PIGS

A particularly odd archaeological feature is probably connected to hunting. There are ditched and banked enclosures or avenues called cursuses all over Ireland and Britain that seem to have developed out of enclosures connected to long-barrow burial sites. British cursuses mostly date from the mid-fourth to early third millennium BC and range in length from fifty metres to as much as ten kilometres. Many were altered or lengthened, some were in use for over a thousand years and sometimes one end of the cursus was more substantial, with high banks and wooden palisading.

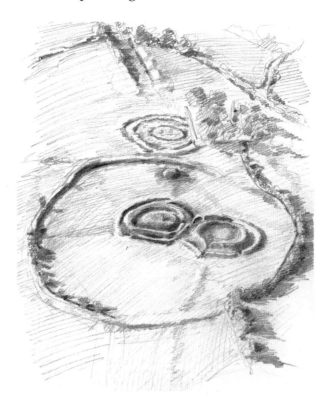

Tara, Co. Meath. The cursus visible in the upper part of the image is now called the Banqueting House. The circular earthworks in the foreground are known as Cormac's House, the Royal Seat and the Mound of the Hostages.

Animals were possibly driven along these cursuses for marksmen to test their skills: many arrowheads turn up near the ends of some. Similar alleyways lined with temporary barriers were used in Europe in more recent times to drive wild prey towards hunters. Fine stone weapons, long barrows, human or animal bones and skulls, henges and unusual burials all appear near these cursuses, indicating that many different activities happened in their vicinity.[32]

Events staged at these cursuses must have demonstrated an elite's power, much as happened at Roman arenas and Spanish bullrings. Some British cursuses were still in use in the Bronze Age, but the Irish ones are undated. They are mostly short, and occur at important sites like Crúachan, Newgrange, Loughcrew and Tara (now misleadingly called the Banqueting Hall) and their banks could have made excellent grandstands. The Irish cursuses all lead up slopes towards the main centres of the sites, while the lower ends descend into boggy or watery places. There are no known votive offerings from the wet areas, but perhaps this wet ground was chosen to stop animals, or people, escaping.

Irish folk stories often attribute prehistoric earthworks to the activities of gigantic pigs and worms. One is therefore called the Worm's Ditch, while the Crúachan cursus is 'the Mucklaghs' from *mucluch*, a piggery. As pigs nuzzle along they leave parallel furrows behind them like miniature earthworks and so monstrous pigs supposedly dug out many Irish earthworks. It could also be that wild boar were an actual prey in these cursuses; vicious when cornered, they make fearsome opponents for any huntsmen.

Modern pig of Iron Age type, from Kilballyowen, Co. Limerick. Folklore attributes many large prehistoric earthworks to the work of gigantic pigs.

BRONZE

The smiths, meanwhile, were trying to make metal weapons or tools, hardening copper with the arsenic that often accompanies the ore. As arsenic is highly toxic, the workers' health would have often suffered without much improvement in the metal, but around 2000 BC they learnt that if tin is added, the result is bronze.[33]

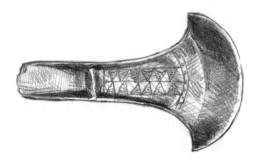

Bronze axe, Co. Fermanagh.

The arrival of bronze technology in Ireland *c.*2000 BC marked the real end of the Stone Age. Bronze weapons and tools were twice as robust as flint ones and generally replaced them, though flint knapping continued for specific purposes such as arrowheads. Bronze had first developed in the Middle East a thousand years earlier, but tin was originally mined in Afghanistan and Anatolia, so for a long period bronze production got no further west than Crete and Hungary. Astonishingly, the next production centres were Ireland and Britain. It seems the sailing routes brought Mediterranean metalworkers here when the Cornish tin field was found, and, as in the eastern Mediterranean, little faience beads were now made in Britain and Ireland, with the magical ingredients of bronze, copper and tin incorporated into their glaze.[34]

Irish copper smiths were proficient, and so an Irish bronze industry developed using Cornish tin. New metal-working communities grew up, and although the genetic evidence for Ireland and Cornwall is lacking, DNA analysis reveals that people of Albanian and east Mediterranean stock settled around the north-Welsh Orme promontories, the largest copper mines in prehistoric western Europe. The Albanians were major copper and gold workers, and the eastern Mediterranean provided the bronze technology.[35]

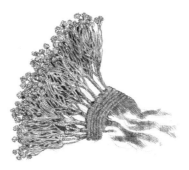

Early-Bronze Age horsehair tassle found in a woollen bag. It had been left in a pond used for ritual offerings near Armoy, Co. Antrim.

Irish smiths were soon making superbly decorated bronze battle-axes and these travelled to mainland Britain and up the Great Glen to eastern Scotland, Denmark and Germany. Bronze tools were also made, and the country's first town, Corrstown, arose near the north-Antrim coast.[36] A couple of centuries later, the European burial practice changed to individual cremations, and the Irish followed suit. Bodies were burned on large pyres and the ashes put in Beaker pottery vessels or cists, though in some places such as at Ballykeel portal tomb in County Armagh inhumations in cists continued. A henge at Dún Ruadh in Tyrone was also remodelled. In the middle there was a cobbled area with a cobbled pathway leading to it and a horseshoe-shaped cairn heaped up around it. About a dozen cist burials were dug into the cairn.

Earlier cist burials were inhumations, but a few centuries later cremation became the norm. Normally, each cist contained the remains of one adult, sometimes accompanied by a child.

Such elaborate burial practices were only for important people. Most of Europe, Ireland included, was now a patchwork of warrior-ruled territories. Men fought with bows and arrows, javelins and daggers, all requiring skill, fitness and training. In richer areas, such as Wessex and parts of Germany, great men had their possessions placed around them in large tombs, but the Irish had simpler traditions. Their burials were under stone mounds like megalithic cairns that stood on hill ridges and included just a few rare or magical objects: a bronze weapon, archery equipment, some gold finery, amber necklaces, jet buttons, faience beads or a bronze razor blade.[37]

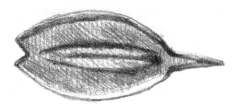

Bronze razors are often found in cist burials, suggesting that being clean-shaven was a mark of status.

There were also several richer Irish burials. A skeleton found in a cave near Castlemartyr in County Cork in 1806 was dressed in a 'garment' of oval gold plates sewn together with gold wire, and wore an amber necklace. Only one amber bead and a small gold plate now survive (one of the Cork jewellers who acquired the rest proudly said he melted down 'half a coal box' of gold plate) but its repoussé herringbone patterns indicate an early-Bronze Age date. It must have been as rich a garment as the early-Bronze Age golden Mold Cape from Wales (now in the British Museum).

This small gold plate and amber bead are all that remain of the richest Irish early-Bronze Age burial, found in Knockane Cave near Castlemartyr, Co. Cork, in 1806.

Another way to mark important Bronze Age graves was the raising of single standing stones beside the burial cists. There are many early-Neolithic standing stones in Armorica, and some Irish ones possibly date from this time, but the tallest are Bronze Age and stand on the Curragh in County Kildare. Their cists were plundered long ago, but one had an archer's wrist guard in it when excavated. Another stands at the centre of an earth-banked henge called Longstone Rath. Its cist held the remains of two people, cremated on a large pyre that scarred the cist's stones and left a thick layer of ash. There are several others with early-Bronze Age burials at their feet.

Standing stone, Punchestown, Co. Kildare. It is 7m high and the tallest of the three Curragh standing stones by several metres. An empty cist lay at its feet.

You stone at Aonach Pataoin
Beneath you lie three good young men.
Patan son of Muir níocht's king
Is the most prized hero in this grave.

Oh stone of Sliabh Chklláin Chruaidh
To which our hosts would march,
Beside you died a hero
Collán of the thick feet.

Oh stone in gleaming Grian
That Maoil Eanaigh raised in early times
You stand with no shame
Over red-faced Dáire's son.

(From 'The Stones of Ireland' in the *Duanaire Finn* [1626–7],
translated by Gerard Murphy.[38])

Each verse refers to a different stone. One in County Louth supported the
mortally wounded Cú Chulainn so he could fight on to his last breath, the Stone
of the Tree in County Limerick is part of a spirit tree in a nearby lough and
others have holes in them through which young women passed newborn babies
to give them strength, or people shook hands when oath-taking.

*The Hole Stone, Doagh, Co. Antrim. Young
couples pledged their troth by clasping hands
through the hole, which was carved through
the stone in prehistoric times.*

ON THE MOVE

Bronze Age wagons and boats facilitated mobility, but most people lived and died close to where they were born. One odd consequence of this is that there are many 'recumbent' stone circles in southwest Ireland and in Aberdeenshire in northeast Scotland, but nowhere else. They are all oriented to the furthest southwest settings of the moon or the sun. Many henges and Irish-style cist burials also arose in the Inverness–Aberdeen region and analysis of tooth enamel from one reveals that this individual lived in County Antrim as a child, so the Bronze Age Irish must have come and amalgamated their traditions with those of northeastern Scotland.

Irish settlement in the Inverness–Aberdeen region facilitated gift-and-exchange trading. Quantities of Baltic amber reached Ireland, and the many boat images incised on Scandinavian rocks testify to their importance. Jet from Whitby also reached Ireland; a burial with a superb jet necklace on Bute marks a western point on these trade routes, while the gold-covered body with the amber necklace in a County Cork cave lay at their southern end.

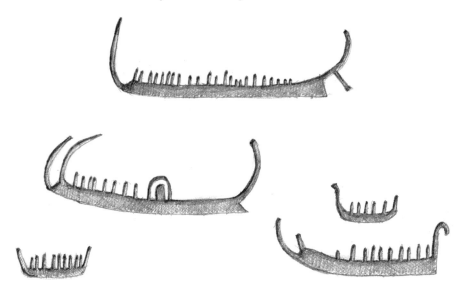

Part of a fleet of Bronze Age boats carved on a rock outcrop at Hornness, Skjeborg, Norway. Thousands of boat images were carved along the Scandinavian coastline from about 1750 BC when the Bronze Age reached the area.

Bronze Age rock carving at Derrynablaha, Co. Kerry. Exposed rocks were selected for similar carvings all along the Atlantic Fringe during this period. Only those of the British Isles are entirely abstract, and possibly, like the carvings on megalithic tombs, represent hallucinatory experiences.

Northeast Ulster's advantageous position in this communications chain meant that it received a higher input from northern Britain and Europe than other regions. Many Beaker Culture accoutrements, including archery equipment and conical jet buttons, are more often found here than elsewhere, and their shapes and styles resemble those of southwestern Scotland. Northeast Ulster's unusual prosperity was vividly demonstrated by the discovery of the mid-Bronze Age settlement of Corrstown near Portrush in County Antrim in 2001. Its wide, cobbled street had twenty-nine roundhouses on either side, with flagstone pathways leading to them. There were cobbled side streets and larger, more prosperous houses stood in the centre with drainage gullies and elaborate entrances. A large stone macehead in one of the bigger houses and a decorated pot buried at the entrance of another hint at the community's life and rituals. This little town was unique in northern Europe, comparable only to the fortified towns of southern Iberia, France and Italy, but in an outrageous act of cultural terrorism, only a speedy 'rescue' excavation was allowed before it was bulldozed to make way for a housing development.[39]

Bronze Age cultural communications also led to the appearance of cup and ring marks incised into exposed rocks along the Atlantic Fringe and Mediterranean. The Irish and British examples generally appear near tracks leading across the hills, and their circular designs and channels were probably meant to direct magical pools of rain water.[40] There are similar carvings in Armorica and Galicia, more in northern Italy and a few in Greece. In southern Iberia and Italy, the carvings depict warriors in horned helmets surrounded by Bronze Age martial finery and wagons, while in Scandinavia the carvings are of fleets of boats and horn-helmeted warriors. Bull horns were important emblems of authority and power in Bronze Age societies.

Rock carving showing a wagon drawn by oxen, and people from southern Spain, a memorial of the new culture that transformed European society in the Bronze Age.

COMETS AND VOLCANOES

Bronze rapier, c.1200 BC, from Lissane, Co. Derry. This superb piece of bronze casting is 79.7cm long.

The vicissitudes of nature were never far away. In 1628 BC, the Aegean volcanic island of Santorini erupted, causing destruction and disruption in the eastern Mediterranean. It threw a massive plume of dust into the upper atmosphere. Once again sunlight was reduced, and even the bristlecone pine-tree rings in California record a severe frost the following year, something that only happened on one other occasion, in 207 BC. There was little tree growth in Ireland for several years, and few signs of settlements thereafter, suggesting another famine and population collapse.

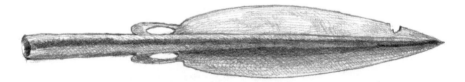

Middle-Bronze Age spearhead.

Irish metalworkers ceased to be leaders in their field, and instead imitated the weaponry of wealthy Wessex. Throughout the Middle Bronze Age they produced spears and javelins with more sophisticated blades and also made rapiers, the earliest swords, with blades up to eighty centimetres long. On Tara's Mound of the Hostages the burials became cremations in urns with only a few personal ornaments, as was happening in Europe. One Tara urn burial included a large bronze dagger and a superb polished stone axehead, suggesting a person of exceptional importance, and the last burial here was equally significant. Under a heavy slab lay the uncremated body of a youth wearing an amulet of bronze, amber, jet and faience beads, rare objects from Britain and the Baltic with magical and healing properties. The burial is radiocarbon-dated c.1350 BC.

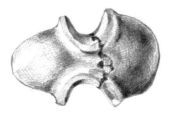

Axehead from a Bronze Age urn burial at Tara, Co. Meath.

*An Irish version of an Urnfield burial at
Tallaght, Co. Dublin.*

Almost seven hundred years after the Santorini explosion, another catastrophe struck in 1159 BC. This time sunlight was weakened for eighteen years and the unusual trace elements in the ice cores suggest that a cometary near miss had left large amounts of its dust in the upper atmosphere. Comet fragments may have hit the earth, and some Irish myths sound like folk memories: the legendary invaders of Ireland, the Tuatha Dé Danann, arrived out of the sky after covering the earth in darkness and fog and hurling down fire and blood; the great god Lugh came out of the western sky, his face brighter than the sun and his shining arm raised before him; while the Irish god Balar, who is closely associated with Lugh, appeared with a 'venomous fiery eye' that threw out lightning bolts. This eye also had seven coverings. 'When the first cover was removed the bracken withered; with the second the grass became copper coloured; removing the third made the woods heat up, after the fourth smoke came out of the trees; with the fifth everything glowed red, the sixth made sparks fly, and with the seventh the forests caught fire.'[41]

Whether any of these tales actually relate to the 1159 BC event is impossible to say, but it caused upheavals across the globe. China had a run of crop failures and famines,and the semi-urbanized societies of Greece, Anatolia, Egypt and the Middle East collapsed as the rains failed. Nearly all the fifty known eastern Mediterranean major sites were destroyed or fell into ruin. In Ireland and Britain, agriculture collapsed, meaning that livestock, fish and deer were once again the most dependable sources of nutrition.[42]

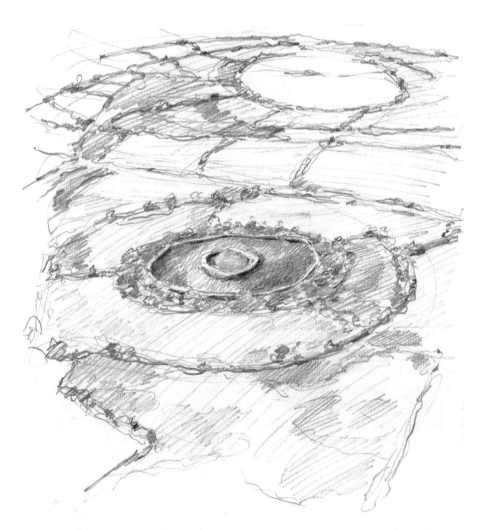

Rathgall hill fort, Co. Wicklow. In the late Bronze Age there was a circular ditch 16m in diameter, a large circular house, several cremated burials and the site of a funeral pyre. This site later became a capital seat of the Leinster kings, and is one of the few identified settlements of the late-Bronze Age period in Ireland. The dry stone walls were added in the Iron Age.

Ireland took well over a hundred years to recover, but during this period many defendable retreats – artificial islands called crannogs, as well as huge hill forts – were created, requiring command of a large labour force. Similar hill forts appeared all over northern Europe, and new burial customs were adopted. The ashes were placed in urns without grave goods and buried in cemeteries, leading to this society being dubbed the Urnfield Culture. Analysis shows that the Irish dead were cremated on extremely hot pyres that needed large quantities of timber. Afterwards, the bones were collected and pulverized. There was no uniformity to Irish customs, however, and older burial traditions were sometimes practised cheek by jowl with the new ones.

A socketed axehead from the Dowris hoard of the eighth century BC (Co. Offaly), a product of the improved late-Bronze Age casting techniques originally developed in the Middle East.

Around the time of the 1159 BC disaster, several hoards were buried in the ground to be later recovered, a useful precaution in troubled times. A bronze smith in County Kildare, for instance, hid his goods in a hole. As well as his tools of trade, an anvil, a vice, a chisel and a saw, there were marketable goods, including state-of-the-art weapons such as socketed axeheads produced by core-casting. This was a technique only recently introduced from northern Europe.

The most remarkable site of the period is Emhain Macha, Navan, the legendary royal capital of Ulster. It was a purely ritual site, but a circular fort built a kilometre away on a hill was inhabited and has a calibrated radiocarbon date of *c.*1100 BC. It had three concentric rings of V-shaped ditches, which were standard defensive structures at the time, and it was undoubtedly a high-status site. The skulls of the two largest prehistoric dogs from the British Isles were found here, as well as the bones of some unusually large cattle and a particularly long goat horn. There were also saddle querns, charred barley, and the residues of bronze and gold casting. Nearby, a 4-metre-deep, 25-metre-wide ritual pond (now called the King's Stables) was dug and whole animal carcasses thrown in along with red deer antlers, sword moulds and the severed facial features of a human skull.

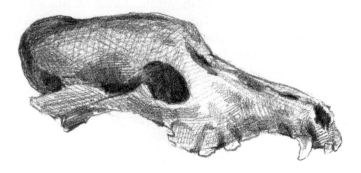

A Bronze Age-period dog's skull found at Haughey's Fort near Emhain Macha, Navan, Co. Armagh.

At Ralaghan, Co. Cavan, a totem figure found in a bog has a hole presumably for an erect penis (now missing), and is the only cult image of this period.[43] Few traces of ordinary Irish people are found in the two hundred years after 1159 BC, however. A high number must have died in this ecological crisis.

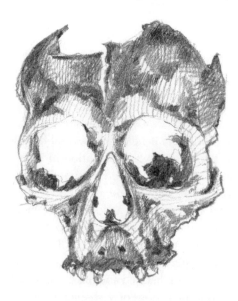

Face section of a head found in the Navan ritual pond now called the King's Stables.

The Ralaghan yew-wood figure was
found in 1908 in a bog near Taghart
Mountain, Co. Cavan. Quartz grains
found in the hole probably held the
missing penis in place.

HERDERS, WAGONS AND HORSES

There were other consequences to this long period of cultural change and ecological crises. The original Indo-European language, ancestor of Irish, English, Greek, Sanskrit, Slavonic, Latin and others, was probably spoken by the first farmers in Anatolia and accompanied the Neolithic expansion across Eurasia, gradually changing into different dialects and languages as it went. One of these, spoken by cattle-herding pastoralists on the Pontic Steppes in the Ukraine, had words for salient features of their culture, including horses, sheep, metal, wagons, axles and wheels, for they had domesticated horses and wool-bearing sheep from further east, copper and gold from the Danube basin, and wagons inspired by those of Mesopotamia.

Stone engraved with the image of a man with spear, wagon, shield and sword from southern Spain. The round object with a handle is probably a bronze mirror from Cyprus. These are the accoutrements of a Bronze Age man of power.

The natural disasters of the third and second millennia BC encouraged this culture's spread. While harvest failures destroyed crop-dependent communities, pastoralists could largely live from their stock, and horses or ox-drawn wagons gave freedom of movement. Chieftainly elites emerged, whose wealth and power depended upon herds, horses and weaponry, and versions of this way of life were practised across Eurasia by the end of the second millennium BC. Like many other Indo-European tongues Irish has words reflecting these changes, such as Indo-European *ekwos, Irish *each*, a horse, *rot-o, roth, a wheel, *reg, rí, a king with sacred and ritual powers, and *teuta, tuath, a tribal military unit.

By 2000 BC, these warrior-herdsmen had also invented the horse-drawn war chariot, the fastest fighting tool of the time. It dominated warfare for the next 1500 years and encouraged further cultural expansion, leading to the Greek-speaking Mycenaean society that ruled Greece after the Santorini volcanic explosion.

In southern Iberia, carved stones memorialize these warrior-herdsmen. They are surrounded by swords, conical helmets (often horned), round shields, javelins and four-wheeled carts. They also often show another wonder of the time, bronze mirrors from Cyprus, whose reflections were thought to be portals to spirit dimensions. Slashing swords also now appear. In the Middle East, it was found that if lead were added to the bronze mix, it became viscous and malleable, allowing the molten metal to pour into more complex moulds and have sharper blades.

As lead bronze was malleable, sheet bronze could also be made. Hammered bronze cauldrons, shields, trumpets, helmets and body armour all came into use, and soon became essential possessions for men of power throughout Europe, Ireland included.

Flesh hook from Dunaverney, Co. Antrim. Thirty-six flesh hooks are known from the Atlantic Fringe. They are thought to have been designed for chieftainly feasting, with joints of meat dangling from them into cauldrons. Great importance was placed upon which pieces of meat were given to whom.

Bronze sword from the Dowris hoard, Co. Offaly. The addition of lead to the bronze in the late Bronze Age allowed the production of slashing swords with sharp edges.

A lead-bronze cauldron from Ballyscullion, Co. Antrim.

Wonderful cauldrons often feature in Irish tales about chieftains' feasts. They were rare, so large, rough pottery vessels were also used. An improved breed of horse from the Pontic Steppes also arrived and archery fell from favour as mounted warriors now fought with lances, slashing swords and round shields. Most surviving Irish shields are thin bronze and meant for show, although one sturdy leather shield does exist. Nordic influences also appear, a consequence of the Irish elite's thirst for Baltic amber.

Bronze Age leather shield found at Clonbrin, Co. Long-ford, and presented to the Royal Irish Academy in 1908. It is the only one of its kind ever to be found in Europe. Wooden moulds for shaping leather shields have been found in counties Mayo and Antrim.

Another peculiarly Irish development was the *fulacht fiadh*, horseshoe-shaped mounds of stones beside stone-lined pits. Intense fires heated up these stones that were dropped into water-filled pits to bring them up to a high temperature. These are usually said to be cooking sites but as no butchered bones are found, it is much more likely that they were mainly used for washing. In the flea- and lice-ridden conditions of the time, hot pools in which humans could wash themselves and purge their clothes would have been a great luxury.

THE LANGUAGE OF TRADE

The Dark Age caused by the 1159 BC event finally lifted when new metal prospectors appeared c.1000 BC. These incomers had ties to the kingdom of Tartessos in southwestern Iberia and probably also caused a linguistic transformation. The Atlantic Celtic tongues of Ireland, Brittany and Britain are peculiar, because although their vocabulary is Indo-European the grammar has totally alien features. These include changing the first consonants of words to denote case, gender and tense, and using locutions to express activity and status. Only the Semitic tongues of north Africa and the eastern Mediterranean share these features, and this remarkable Semitic-Indo-European linguistic amalgamation apparently happened in Tartessos.[44]

The name of the Tartessian deity Lokobo was inscribed in the local script on a stone in southwestern Spain. In due course he became the Irish god Lugh.

Tartessos's wealth grew because its fleets, entrepreneurs and emporia collected, processed and traded produce from the Atlantic Fringe and north Africa with the Semitic cultures of the Near East. They badly needed bronze, as the old trade routes for Afghan tin broke down after the 1159 BC disaster, so Irish bronze and Cornish tin were in high demand. The Bible records how great fleets from 'wealthy Tarshish' arrived in the Near East every three years, laden with bronze, gold, silver, apes and peacocks.

Thanks to their contacts with the eastern Mediterranean, the Tartessians developed western Europe's first script. The sub-Mycenaean syllabic script of Cyprus and the proto-alphabets of the Phoenicians inspired the Tartessians, whose inscriptions capture the birth of Atlantic Celtic. They have dedications both to the Semitic goddess Astarte and to Lokobo, the Celtic god Lugus. This creole then spread north with its professional people, traders and metalworkers, so Lokobo became Irish Lugh, the inventor of crafts, protector of travellers and provider of wealth. The name derived from proto-Celtic *lugio*, an oath, so Lokobo began as the god invoked for contracts.

Lugh was also the god of harvests, and his harvest festival, Lughnasa, was celebrated with games, contests, oath-taking, matchmaking and berry collecting. The greatest Lughnasa celebrations were at Tailtu (Teltown) in Meath, later presided over by the Irish high kings.

A memorial slab engraved with an inscription in Tartessian script and a figure from southwestern Spain.

BRONZE AGE BELIEFS

Irish legends often feature Iberian connections. One of them concerns Míl, a Spanish king's son who landed with his men in southwest Ireland and defeated the Tuatha Dé Danann. As this story was composed in Christian times, it gives a partially biblical explanation for the Irish language's creole origins: Míl descended from an Egyptian ruler called Gaedhil Glas, who cobbled together the Irish language from the tongues that God had imposed upon the Tower of Babel's builders to stop them understanding each other.

The Iberian proto-Celts saw a mystical significance in thirds, so their society had three classes – priests, warrior horsemen and herder cultivators – and their deities had tripartite natures. Irish gods and goddesses also had three forms, hence the stone head from Corleck Hill in Cavan with its three faces. As the world's first horse-riding society, the Indo-Europeans also had a horse cult from which was spun the legend of pregnant Macha racing against the Ulster king's horses.

A horse also features in the seventh-century legends about St Patrick's confrontations with king Dáire of Armagh. (His name is an epithet of the Daghdha, the Irish Celtic form of the Indo-European god who became Deus in Latin and Deva in Sanskrit. Armagh's main tribe were called the Dáirine after their god-ancestor.) Dáire gave Patrick, with some prevarication, a great cauldron of foreign workmanship. Soon after this, Patrick killed Dáire's stallion with a curse for grazing on his church's land and made Dáire mortally ill before restoring him and his stallion back to health. Dáire then presented his old ritual hill, Armagh, to Patrick. Interestingly, Dáire's cauldron also sounds like the Daghdha's legendary cauldron, which he took from the invading Tuatha Dé Danann and always contained enough to satisfy a hungry man.

In spite of the country's Christianization, horse-cult customs survived into the Middle Ages, as Giraldus Cambrensis reveals in his description of a thirteenth-century inauguration:

> Among the Kenelcunil there is a certain tribe which is wont to install a king over itself by an excessively abominable and savage ritual. In the presence of all the people of this land in one place a white mare is brought into their midst. Thereupon, he who is to be elevated steps forward in a beastly fashion and exhibits all his bestiality. Right thereafter the mare is killed and boiled piecemeal in water, and in the same water a bath is prepared for him. He gets into the bath and eats of the flesh that is brought to him. When this is done right his rule and sovereignty are consecrated.[45]

Prosperous farmers buried horse skulls under their house floors until the twentieth century, with the explanation that they made music sweet and put a spring in the dancers' steps. Many other ancient Irish beliefs were transformed in the Bronze Age cultural melting pot, and their ritual centres remained powerful places.

The Indo-Europeans' bull cult, for example, represented human origins as coming from a primordial divine cow, and in Ireland this idea combined with earlier myths to create Bóinn, the sky-cow goddess, who is held within Newgrange and is impregnated by the Daghdha. Fragments of another proto-Indo-European sky myth are also embedded in Irish culture. The planet Mercury, the wandering star that appears at sunrise or sunset and was first recorded as a messenger god by the Babylonians, is Budh in early Irish, an Indo-European word meaning victorious or enlightened. The planet is also Budh in Sanskrit, suggesting that the name is a remnant of some ancient concept. The Irish midsummer month that preceded Lugh's festival was also dedicated to Budh and in Sanskrit the word gives us *buddhi,* mind, and Buddha, the enlightened one. Old Irish even had a related epithet for Orion's Belt – Buaile an Bhodhaigh – the Belt of Enlightenment.[46]

The Middle-Bronze Age sun chariot from Trundholm, Denmark, has gold on one side of the iron disk. A sun chariot drawn by horses is found in Irish and Scandinavian myths, and also in the Rigveda.

A GOLDEN AGE

*Late-Bronze Age gold collar from
Clonshin, Co. Clare.*

*Late-Bronze Age gold earring from
Caslterea, Co. Roscommon.*

Thanks to Tartessos, Ireland prospered. Quantities of gold and bronze objects
were produced and there was a spectacular rise in their quality. There were
clear rivalries between the gold-rich south and the warrior north. Even their
feasting bowls and ceremonial trumpets had distinctive forms, and the only gold
objects much used in the north were finely worked clothing fasteners. Virtually all the rest came from the south. These craftsmen made weighty gold torcs
imitating continental designs, hair ornaments, bracelets and earrings based on
Near Eastern shapes, including heavy collars with Phoenician-style decorations,
and gold hair and tress rings identical to Egyptian ones.

*Cast bronze trumpets from Kerry and Antrim
showing the different shapes used in the late
Bronze Age in the north and south of Ireland.*

*Late-Bronze Age Ulster gold
clothes fastener from Clones,
Co. Monaghan.*

The boom lasted about two hundred years. Many trees were felled, in part for metal processing, for over two-thirds of all Irish prehistoric gold comes from this period. One County Clare gold hoard was so large that it filled seventeen turf barrows. The climate became warmer, the population grew and agriculture recovered. Crops were again as important as cattle, large fields were ploughed by oxen, wheeled wagons appeared and better bronze tools were made. New crops were introduced. Bitter vetch, poppies, millet, oats and rye all entered the repertoire, and linseed and flax were reintroduced.

The earliest wheels found in Ireland date from the late Bronze Age. This example, from Doogarymore, Co. Roscommon, was one of a pair buried at a territorial boundary.

A seventh-century BC Irish bucket left in a small lake at Capecastle townland near Armoy, Co. Antrim. Like the Dowris-hoard bucket it had been much used and repaired.

Around 800 BC, this prosperity collapsed. There was a steep fall in the Near East's demand for bronze, as tin and copper mining began in Etruria, the trade route to Afghanistan reopened and iron came into use. A bronze hoard with many Irish spearheads was left in the sea at Huelva, Tartessos's main port, but its wealth did not return. An earthquake and a tsunami possibly devastated the area; indeed Plato's story of the destruction of Atlantis, which he placed near Gadir (Cadiz) beyond the Pillars of Hercules, may in part derive from this disaster.

Be that as it may, around the time of Tartessos's collapse the Phoenicians founded Gadir and became the Atlantic Fringe's main traders. Most of the goods they needed for the Near East came from Iberia and Morocco, however, so their interest in the further reaches of the Atlantic Fringe dwindled. As at Huelva, bronze hoards were left in Ireland's wet places to appease the spirits. Some contact continued with northern Europe. A late-eighth-century BC bronze hoard from County Offaly, the Dowris hoard, includes a much repaired, fifty-year-old bucket from central Europe. The Urnfield Culture staged rituals in which symbolic objects like gold sun disks and bronze buckets surrounded by model birds were carried on miniature bronze wagons, and the Dowris bucket was one of these.

Local versions of Urnfield rituals must have been practised. An Irish copy of the Dowris bucket was deposited in a small lake near Armoy in County Antrim and there were fragments of several other Irish Urnfield buckets in the hoard. They were all packed in a large cauldron along with some state-of-the-art slashing swords, horn-shaped trumpets, and objects shaped like bull testicles. These and the trumpets might relate to a bull cult. Bulls feature in many Irish myths and epics and, intriguingly, an Iron Age stone figure, the Tandragee idol, wears a helmet with two horn stumps, the only known representation of an Irish horned helmet.[47]

The Tandragee idol. Stumps of what are probably horns are visible on the helmet. It was found in a bog near Newry, Co. Down, in the early nineteenth century.

LEAN TIMES

With the bronze trade gone, Ireland fell into a long decline that was exacerbated by another climatic downturn. In the fifth century BC, the weather patterns shifted to colder and wetter conditions, agriculture again came to a virtual halt, and there was another population collapse. There is little sign of any ordinary human activity for several centuries.

Nonetheless, amber and jet continued to arrive and high-quality weapons and armour were forged, but the elite still lived in roundhouses, although their peers elsewhere in Europe now had substantial dwellings. The roundhouses mostly had double walls of wicker with bracken crammed between them and needed frequent replacement, though some were sturdier. On Islandmagee in County Antrim, one had two-metre-thick earthen walls and a wooden plank floor, making it solid and snug.

The hill-fort capital of the Leinster kings at Rathgall in Wicklow, by contrast, only had a wicker roundhouse standing in a ditched compound. Its high status is indicated by the quantities of domestic pottery found here, as pottery had generally ceased to be used in Ireland. In addition, there were hundreds of clay moulds for casting bronze swords, spearheads and axes, and a few faience beads. Their rarity (and magical properties) were such that one bead was incorporated in a gold pendant.[48] There was also a saddle quern for milling, suggesting the king benefitted from grain production, and under the roundhouse's floor there was a human burial with a penannular gold bead nestling amongst the bones. Perhaps this was the founder of the Leinster dynasty.

This burial deposit of cremated bones and a gold ring was found below the centre of the Iron Age roundhouse at Rathgall, Co. Wicklow, the capital seat of later Leinster kings.

III. *The Age of Iron*

The Age of Iron

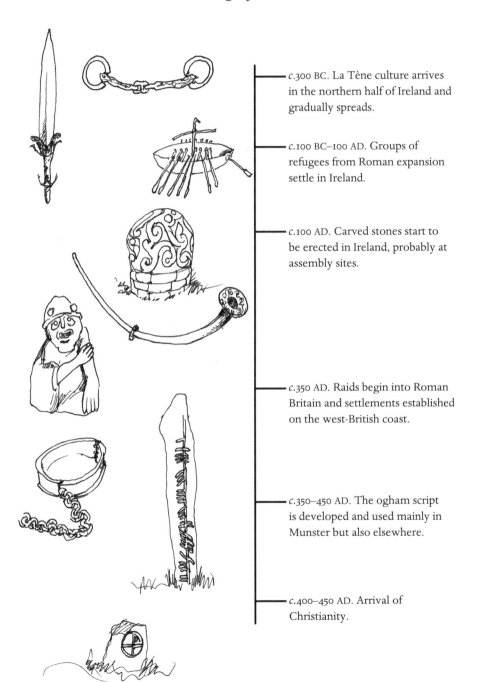

*c.*300 BC. La Tène culture arrives in the northern half of Ireland and gradually spreads.

*c.*100 BC–100 AD. Groups of refugees from Roman expansion settle in Ireland.

*c.*100 AD. Carved stones start to be erected in Ireland, probably at assembly sites.

*c.*350 AD. Raids begin into Roman Britain and settlements established on the west-British coast.

*c.*350–450 AD. The ogham script is developed and used mainly in Munster but also elsewhere.

*c.*400–450 AD. Arrival of Christianity.

IRON AND CHARIOTS

New technologies transformed central Europe. Urnfield society evolved into the Hallstatt culture that brought iron production to the west. Substantially different methods are needed for iron production than for bronze, and the Hallstatt people grew rich supplying Greeks, Phoenicians and Etruscans with iron and salt, gold and amber, and tin and copper. Their hilltop citadels emulated Mediterranean cities and palaces, and their dead chieftains were laid out on iron-sheathed chariots surrounded by their finest Greek possessions, including Attic Red-Figure drinking vessels and large bronze urns. The Hallstatt culture made little impact on Ireland, however. Just a few iron tools and weapons were made, presumably by immigrant smiths, and about fifty Irish bronze swords that mimic Hallstatt iron ones.

In the fifth century BC, the Hallstatt culture gave way to La Tène, which also traded with the Greeks and Etruscans but was more aggressive. It built sophisticated hilltop fortresses rather than palaces, and its chieftains were buried with weapons and war chariots. Superb craftsmen made martial finery, fusing Etruscan, Greek, Oriental and local elements into the La Tène style that is now closely associated with the Celts.

The lure of riches ultimately caused mass migrations. La Tène tribes invaded Greece, Anatolia and northern Italy, where territorial struggles led to Etruria's collapse and Rome's rise. Some even headed to Britain. In east Yorkshire there are cemeteries of grave mounds covering La Tène chieftains laid on chariots and wearing impressive personal finery, yet bone analysis reveals that most of them were locals. It looks as if a small La Tène group arrived in Yorkshire from the continent, where it joined forces with natives who adopted its customs. The other British tribes eagerly adopted La Tène decorative styles and iron production, and a few intrepid adventurers even crossed northern Britain to Ulster. They brought their craftsmen miners and blacksmiths, as their power depended upon their weaponry.

La Tène-period scabbard from Lisnacrogher, Co. Antrim.

La Tène Sites

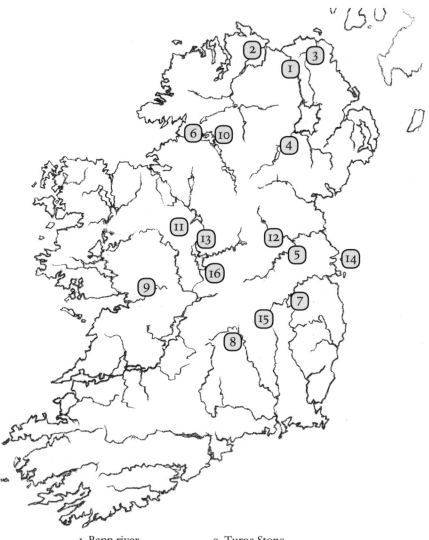

1. Bann river
2. Broighter
3. Lisnacrogher
4. Navan
5. Tara
6. Boa Island
7. Kilcullen/Dún Ailinne
8. Kilkenny
9. Turoe Stone
10. Kiltierney
11. Crúachan
12. Teltown
13. Corlea
14. Lambay Island
15. Freestone Hill
16. Visneach

IRISH LA TÈNE

La Tène-period sword from Lisnacrogher bog, Co. Antrim.

The first Irish La Tène incomers settled in the northeast, lured once again by County Antrim's geology. Above its flint-bearing limestone is a thick layer of basalt containing quantities of iron ore, which the miners and blacksmiths exploited for spear and sword production in particular. Well-made iron sword blades were extremely effective, and could slice off a head or bend a bronze sword with one blow. However, few farming or wood-working iron tools were produced, unlike Britain, where they came into general use and greatly improved tribal prosperity.

The Broighter-hoard torc. It is hollow, a form known both in Britain and continental Europe but not otherwise in Ireland. However, the decoration is typically Irish so it was probably brought into the country and then embellished. The hoard was found 2km northwest of Limavady, Co. Derry, close to the Foyle.

In stark contrast, Ireland showed few signs of social improvement during the Iron Age. In 207 BC, another cometary near miss left another dust veil in the upper atmosphere. Roman authors talk about showers of glowing stones falling from the sky and of the sun losing its brightness and power. There were crop failures and famine from western Europe to China, where 'the stars were not seen for three months', and for only the second time in seven thousand years the bristlecone pines of California were hit by frosts.[49] There was also another Icelandic volcanic eruption in 44 BC, followed by several harvest failures.

In these conditions, famines were frequent. This probably explains why cattle raiding and deer hunting feature so largely in Irish epic tales. The poor might starve, but the aristocracy had a lifestyle to maintain, and meat was at a premium. Most of the open-air *fulacht fiadh* date from this time. The excavators of Dún Ailinne, the royal site in Kildare, found only thirteen barley grains as opposed to nineteen thousand animal bones. Grain was scarce even for kings, but there were piles of hazelnut shells, as this ancient staple was in high demand.

County Antrim remained the hub of La Tène activity for quite a time. Most of its finest objects are votive offerings left in the river Bann. The other major Antrim site was Lisnacrogher, a boggy lake drained in the 1870s. The local peat cutters found numerous La Tène artefacts here, many of superb workmanship, along with heavy wooden beams, stakes and wattles. It had been a ritual site laid out like European ones, with a platform jutting over a lake from which suppli-cants cast precious objects into the water.[50]

Bronze horse bit of c.200–300 AD, from a hoard containing many other horse trappings found at Attymon, Co. Galway. Finely decorated horse bits are amongst the most common La Tène objects found in Ireland: part of the prestigious equipment horse-riding elites.

The La Tène elite ultimately expanded their control across Ulster, Connacht and Meath, which probably explains why the later epics concentrate on these regions. Much of their beautifully wrought equipment had to do with horses, including sculpted bronze bits and chariot fittings, but there were also superbly worked iron swords, elaborately decorated bronze scabbards, long curved bronze trumpets and pieces of ceremonial headgear that were decorative tours de force.

There are only about two dozen Irish La Tène swords, a further indica-tion of how small this elite was, but their votive offerings were impressive. The Broighter hoard from the Foyle included a large continental or south-British gold torc and a gold boat. This has a mast, seven pairs of oars and rowers' benches, and looks much like the larger curraghs, Viking long ships and medieval birlinns that sailed these waters for another two thousand years. The only comparable

Four La Tène trumpets were found in the 1790s at Loughnashade, near Navan, Co. Armagh, but this is the only one to survive. The workmen who uncovered them while digging a ditch said there were many human bones and skulls in the same area.

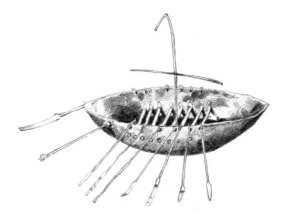

Gold boat from the Broighter hoard, measuring 18.4cm by 7.6c and weighing 85g. It came equipped with benches, rowlocks, two rows of nine oars and a steering paddle as well as grappling tools, three forks, a yardarm and a spear.

La Tène object is a miniature gold log boat with attached paddles from Germany, but the Celts' seagoing boats were in a different category. Their iron technology produced sturdy vessels held together by nails and bolts.

Irish La Tène finery included gold torcs, brooches and drinking vessels, while well-crafted bowls and cauldrons were as essential for their feasts as for their Bronze Age predecessors. The chieftains were effectively living an updated version of the same ethos that had dominated European life for fifteen hundred years. Admittedly, most Irish chariots looked more like farm carts than the technically advanced models of their continental cousins, but they were effective, and there are several elegant pieces of joinery from more sophisticated vehicles.

On reaching fighting age, an Irish youth of the warrior class received spears, a round shield and a chariot. He then had to earn his manhood by killing some adversaries in battle and bringing their heads home. It was the same heroic approach to life as that of the European Celts.

La Tène tankard from Carrickfergus, Co. Antrim. It was probably brought in from Gaul in the first century AD.

Irish La Tène society followed many other continental customs, including leaving bodies in bogs. The victims were often healthy people from the higher levels of society, and all had met violent ends. One recent find, 'Old Croaghan Man', consists of the severed torso of a man of excellent physique and over six foot tall that was staked down in a bog with withies. He had uncalloused hands, well-manicured fingernails, and his nipples were slashed. This was done to disempower him, for kissing a man's nipples was an act of subservience, possibly since the days of the gold disks. In his 'Confession', St Patrick records that he refused to suck the nipples of the Irish boatmen who offered to take him to Britain: to make amends he swore a Christian oath of loyalty instead.

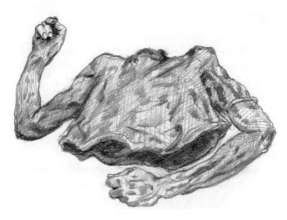

Two bog torsos, 'Old Croghan Man' and 'Clonycavan Man'. They are named after the Meath townlands, about 40km apart, where they were found in 2003.

Another bog body, 'Clonycavan Man', sported a Mohawk haircut, kept upright by a gel made from plant oil and pine resin from southwestern France or Spain, indicating that he too must have come from an affluent level of society. He had been hit at least twice around the head with a stone axe or mace while Old Croaghan Man had been stabbed as well as having his head and lower parts cut off.

An iron axe from Lisnacrogher, Co. Antrim.

CARVED STONES AND ROTARY QUERNS

The Turoe stone, a granite boulder decorated with La Tène patterns, now located near Bullaun village, Co. Galway. Originally it stood about 3km away beside Feerwore rath. An excavation of 1944 indicated that this site dates from c.100 BC–100 AD.

Remarkably few La Tène objects exist in the southern half of Ireland. There are, however, a few impressively carved stones: an egg-shaped stone from Cavan, a phallic-shaped one near a megalithic tomb in Roscommon, and the Turoe stone, from a hill fort in Galway. The unornamented phallic Lia Fáil or Stone of Destiny at Tara is another. During a new king's inauguration rites he had to drive his chariot hard against it to make its axle scream.

Around the first century AD, rotary querns reached Ireland. This improved method of grain milling was developed in Europe around 500 BC and replaced the saddle quern, the back-breaking method used since Neolithic times. A disk-like upper stone (the 'hand stone') was rotated on a lower stone with the help of a wooden handle. The Celtic tribes of the Atlantic Fringe made beehive querns, with the upper stones domed like beehives, and these reached Ulster from Scotland.

About two hundred beehive querns come from areas of La Tène rule, but none from elsewhere, so their distribution reflects a cultural division. A handful have their outer surfaces carved in a simplified La Tène style (stone carving was an Irish idiosyncrasy), and most surviving examples were unused votive offerings left in watery places.

Later, the simpler form of the rotary quern with its disk-shaped upper-hand stone arrived from maritime western Scotland and became the tool of a new social phenomenon. As independent landowners asserted their position in tribal Ireland, grain production increased, and these hand-turned rotary querns were in demand all over the country.

Beehive quern from Ticooly-O'Kelly, Co. Galway. There are about two hundred beehive querns but only a few are decorated, in a simplified La Tène style.

IRON AGE MONUMENTS

The Iron Age elite revered ancient sacred places. In the first century AD, a new ditch was dug round the megalithic passage tomb of Kiltierney in Fermanagh, and nineteen cremated burials were inserted into the lower edges of its cairn at regularly spaced intervals, each covered with its own mound. Elsewhere, new ring barrows appeared, imitating earlier burial mounds, and the graves often contained relics of the past such as stone axeheads or Bronze Age weapons. At Carrowmore megalithic cemetery in Sligo, wooden structures were built near two of the old tombs and large quantities of unburnt human remains were deposited, mostly skulls and teeth.

They also reworked the old tribal sites. A cemetery of new ring barrows arose at Crúachan, and Tara was targeted, too. Its main site, the Rath of the Synods, was vandalized in 1900–2 by British Israelites looking for the Lost Ark, but recent excavation has revealed that the site began as a Bronze Age burial mound. It was later flattened to let several circular timber structures be built on the site after which a ring fort was raised, enclosing a large roundhouse. Inside there was a number of Roman objects: pieces of Gaulish wine flagons, a goblet, a broken brooch, glass beads and inlay, two iron padlocks, a lead seal and a draughtsman's dividers. Were these the belongings of an Irish king?

The excavation of the Ulster site of Navan or Emhain Macha (Ptolemy's Isamnion) gives a more detailed picture. A figure-of-eight timber enclosure was erected in the early Iron Age with a funnel-shaped avenue leading to its entrance. This was burnt and rebuilt twice, and a second one was put up beside it.

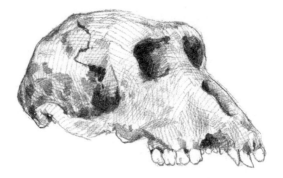

Barbary ape skull. The ape must have come from north Africa and its head was buried under the foundations of a large palisaded complex at Navan, Co. Armagh.

The last of these figure-of-eight structures was burnt and dismantled *c.*100 BC and a vast circular building erected. It had an enormous tree trunk at its centre, perhaps a totem representing the world tree that held up the heavens and had roots deep in the earth. The whole structure was filled with boulders piled up in sections, making a wheel pattern like a symbolic sun. Each section consisted of weathered stones brought from different places, probably from old megalithic tombs. After this, the upper parts of the building were set on fire and the mound was capped with turves. Indeed, the site's name, Emhain, derives from an early Celtic phrase meaning 'sturdy posts'.

Navan's reworking would have enhanced its rulers' status, for the mound now contained a spirit feasting hall like the large megalithic tombs. Its top was flat, making a raised place where the rulers or elite could stand during rituals and fairs. Such was the importance of this place that its name, Emhain Macha, was later used to describe all spirit realms.

There are few La Tène objects from Navan, but a nearby ritual pond, Lough-nashade, which yielded four superb bronze La Tène trumpets in the eighteenth century, along with many human skulls. Even more remarkably, a Barbary ape's skull was buried under one of Navan's timber figure-of-eight palisades. Exotic animals were often presented to royalty all over Europe, and as part of this ape's spinal column was still attached, it must have come here alive.

Enormous linear earthworks were also created south of Navan. They make a non-continuous barrier, which is puzzling, but woods, bogs or mountains may have made the other areas impassable, and as its timbers have the same radio-carbon dates as the central post at Emhain Macha, 95 ± 9 BC, they must be part of the same project.

These earthworks include two big enclosures – the four-kilometre-long Dorsey in south Armagh and the Dun of Drumsna in Roscommon, at a loop in the Shannon. It may be that they were meant to deter cattle-raiding expeditions, which was a major activity of the warrior elite. The *Táin Bó Cuailgne* (*Cattle Raid of Cooley*) describes how Maedhbh, the sovereignty goddess of Connacht and Tara, is depicted as a human queen leading her fighting men against Ulster's King Conchobhar mac Nessa of Navan to do battle over Ireland's two greatest bulls.

Navan and King Conchobhar also feature in ancient Ireland's greatest love story, *Loinges Mac Uislenn* (*The Exile of the Sons of Uisliu*). It opens with a druid prophesying that Deirdre, the unborn daughter of an Ulster chieftain who cried out from her mother's womb, would be exceptionally beautiful but would cause bloody slaughter. King Conchobhar determined to have her for himself, so she was raised in seclusion at Navan. When she grew up she proved to be the most beautiful woman in Ireland, but before Conchobhar could marry her she confessed to her nurse that the man of her desires must have hair as black as the raven she was watching peck at a slaughtered calf in the winter snow, that he should have cheeks as red as the calf's blood, and a body as white as snow. Her nurse said she knew just such a man, a young warrior called Naoise, and Deirdre contrived to meet him.

> 'A fine heifer is passing by,' Naoise commented.
> 'The heifers are always fine,' she said, 'where there are no bulls.'
> 'You have the finest bull of the province, the king of Ulster,' he riposted.
> 'Between the two of you,' she replied, 'I would choose a young bull like yourself.'[51]

She fled with him and his two brothers to Scotland where they stayed until Conchobhar enticed them home. On their return the king had all three brothers killed, forced Deirdre to live with him for a year and then gave her to the warrior who had killed Naoise. The two men forced her into Conchobhair's chariot, and galloped off to the warrior's house, taunting her as they went, so she leant out of the chariot and let her head smash against a rock.

Navan (Emhain Macha), Co. Armagh. Although the epic tales describe Navan as the seat of the Ulster kings it was, in fact, a place of assembly and ritual rather than a royal dwelling.

*Dún Aonghasa, an Iron Age fort on the cliffs of Inishmore in
the Aran Islands.*

The only other certain royal site to be excavated is Dún Ailinne in Kildare,
the royal capital of Leinster. A megalithic tomb stood here, surrounded by a
banked enclosure. A circular dry-stone wall was built round the hilltop in the
Iron Age, which is still four metres high in places, the tallest surviving wall of
pre-Norman Ireland. Around 250 BC, a figure-of-eight structure virtually identical to those at Navan was built in the compound, with a timber-post avenue
leading up to it. A La Tène sword was buried below the amphitheatre's framework in the same way as the ape's skull was buried at Navan, for these swords
were rarities and symbols of high rank.

Two hundred years later there was a new building phase. Two concentric
palisades were built around a circle of large upright posts, and what was possibly
a wooden tower was erected in the middle. Somewhat later, everything was
dismantled, and the area paved over. Thick layers of debris accumulated over
the paving during hundreds of years of open-air feasting. This consisted of the
bones of butchered cattle, sheep, pigs and horses, amongst which were found a
few lost pieces of finery, such as glass beads, bracelets and Roman fibulae.

These extraordinary structures were designed for large gatherings. Dún Ailinne's kings were said to descend from a union between the Daghdha and Bóinn, tying them into the Irish mythological framework, and palisaded avenues also led to circular enclosures at Crúachan, the royal/tribal capital of Connacht. It was said that the greatest fairs in ancient Ireland were held here. Its cemetery was the resting place of kings and heroes, and beneath it lies Oweynagat cave, a powerful entry point to the spirit world. The Morrígan, a triple goddess with power over fighting and fertility, emerges from this cave at Samhain on a chariot pulled by a one-legged chestnut horse.

The circular hilltop enclosure of Raffin in Meath was as carefully designed as Navan or Tara. A nine-metre-diameter roundhouse stood at its centre, a skull burial lay under a round boulder inside the compound and the lack of occupation debris suggests it was a place of ritual activity. Other sites await investigation. Around Cashel, Munster's royal capital in the Christian era, for example, there are several large circular ditched enclosures, one of which certainly dates back to the Bronze Age.

Ancient ritual sites also continued to be venerated. Quantities of silver and gold, either booty or votive offerings from Roman Britain, were left at Newgrange and hundreds of La Tène carvings on shaped slivers of bone lay in a Loughcrew passage grave. There were strong tribal divisions, and even the fortresses proclaim differing identities. In Munster, some have rings of earth ramparts with dry-stone fortresses at the centre, while in the west, forts like Dún Aonghasa on the Aran Islands have *chevaux-des-frises*, barriers of upright rocks, a defensive structure otherwise only found in northern Iberia. The legends about invaders from Galicia might therefore refer to Iberian warrior groups settling in the west of Ireland. By contrast, hill forts on the eastern side of Ireland look like those of western Britain, and other sites had dry-stone ramparts held together by frameworks of wooden beams secured with hundreds of iron nails, a method also used by tribes in Gaul.

La Tène-decorated bone flake from Loughcrew, Co. Meath. About a hundred of these carefully designed flakes were found in a Loughcrew passage grave when it was opened in the 1860s.

COBBLED BOUNDARIES AND BOG ROADS

Corlea bog road or trackway, Co. Longford. The trackway ended on a small island, from which a second one, using about the same amount of timber, continued for another kilometre to dry land on the far side of the bog. They have both been radiocarbon-dated to 147–8 BC.

The use of war chariots and carts in Ireland implies that they could move cross-country fairly freely. There were large areas of open pasture and it is said that five roads ran out across Ireland from Tara. For most of their distance, these were rough and ready tracks, but a fine 22-kilometre cobbled road in County Cork dates from *c.*150 AD. It ran between the Ballyhoura and Nagle hills with deep ditches on either side, a palisade and three forts, controlling movement along the Blackwater Valley. It was an impressive statement of power based on Roman examples; the Antonine Wall across Scotland was probably constructed only ten years earlier.

An early-Irish word for a road was *slighe* (modern Irish *slí*), meaning 'slashed', suggesting they were often ways cut through scrub and undergrowth. Others, called toghers (from *tochar*, a causeway or trackway), were wood constructions laid across bogs. A passage in the eighth- or ninth-century *Wooing of Étaíne* gives an idea of the labour involved:

> Nobody had ever walked onto the bog, but Eochaid ordered his steward to oversee the labour they put into the causeway, so he went. It was as though all the men in the world came to the bog from sunrise to sunset. They piled up all their clothes into a mound so Midir climbed up to its top and watched them pour a forest into the causeway together with its trunks and roots.[52]

Over a hundred wooden trackways lay in Corlea bog in County Longford. Most of them consisted of woven mats lain on piles of brushwood, and many dated from the Bronze Age, but an Iron Age example had heavy timbers and smoothed planks pegged down to make a stable track that was broad enough for chariots or carts. Its planks show little wear, however, and one section was partially burnt and dismantled. Moreover, its heavy timbers lay directly on the bog's surface so the whole structure sank into it soon after it was made. It was as much a mystical offering to the watery otherworld as a road for the living.

Corlea totem effigy, carved onto the end of a 5m-long pole and found amongst timbers supporting the Iron Age Corlea bog trackway, Co. Longford.

Two to three hundred large oak trees were cut down to make Corlea's kilo-metre-long wooden road. Carved posts are often found near these trackways, and a five-metre pole topped with a figure sporting a snouted head and an erect penis was found amongst the Corlea timbers. It is remarkably like the Ralaghan effigy, carved eight hundred years earlier. Similar totems stood near European pools that were chosen for sanctuaries, such as the Gaulish one described by Roman author Lucan in the first century AD:

> A grove never violated during long ages, which with its knitted branches was shut up in the darkened air and the cold shade ... From the black springs water wells up and gloomy images of the gods, rough-hewn from tree trunks stand there ... The people do not frequent it to worship but leave it to the gods.[53]

CLASSICAL VISITORS

A Roman oculist's stamp from a grave at
Golden Bridge, Co. Tipperary.

As the Romans advanced across Gaul and Britain, Ireland became a haven for Celtic refugees. It is suggested that when Caesar conquered the Veneti – a great seafaring tribe on the Brittany coast – some escaped to Ulster. There are promontory forts on the Antrim coast that look suspiciously like the Veneti's strongholds in Brittany, and the Broighter hoard, with its famous gold boat and continental-style torc, could have Veneti origins.

There is better evidence that some of the Brigantes, a west-British tribe, fled to Ireland, for a group of graves on Lambay Island had Roman goods mixed with typical Brigante objects. In general, though, there is only a light scatter of everyday Roman or Romano-British objects across Ireland such as ladles, keys and padlocks, nail cleaners and brooches, and these probably made their way here through trade. Many are concentrated on tribal or royal assembly hills, where the more affluent members of society gathered.

Some Roman authors hint at a military expedition to Ireland in the second century, but if it came, it left no traces. There is an intriguing burial from Stoneyford in County Kilkenny where ashes placed in a glass urn were surrounded by the accoutrements of a Roman lady, including a glass cosmetics phial and a bronze mirror. It is such a 'normal' Roman burial that it suggests the presence of a Roman community, perhaps a trading post. Indeed, the nearby Iron Age hill fort of Freestone has yielded a large number of small Roman objects.

A Roman oculist's stamp, with his name, for marking eye-salve cakes, was also found in a grave in Tipperary. Was this the last resting place of an itinerant Roman eye doctor?

HEADS AND IDOLS

This La Tène-period three-faced head was found c.1855 near Corleck Hill in Co. Cavan. The festival of Lughnasa was celebrated on Corleck Hill until the twentieth century.

The north of Ireland has many carved stone heads dating from this period. The Celts believed that the head housed the human soul and that it continued living there after death, hence the custom of keeping the heads of slaughtered enemies as trophies, or of throwing others into ritual lakes. The stone heads could relate to this belief, and the three-faced stone head from Corleck Hill may well represent a supernatural being. Hundreds of stone heads are also found in La Tène areas of western Europe. The Celtic sanctuary of Roquepertuse in France had a door-shaped structure at its centre with niches carved into its pillars for skulls and stone masks and a double-faced head similar to the Corleck Hill example was found there. Several more come from the nearby sanctuary of Entremont.

There are also several elaborate sculptures in Ulster. On Boa Island in Lough Erne there is a 'Janus' figure, with identical faces, arms and torsos carved back and front, and a smaller, one-sided version comes from nearby Lustymore Island. There are comparable effigies in France and Germany, including the Janus-headed Holzgerlingen statue.

This Janus figure stands in Caldragh graveyard on Boa Island, Lower Lough Erne, Co. Fermanagh, and is one of the most remarkable Iron Age sculptures in Ireland. The island is named after Badb, one of a triad of war-goddess sisters, the others being Macha and Morrígan.

Stone figure now housed in Armagh Cathedral, probably representing the legendary King Labraidh Loingseach, who had horse's ears.

As well as the Lough Erne sculptures, there is also a half-length figure from Tandragee near Newry with a grimacing face glowering under a helmet, while its right hand clutches the top of his left arm. Another, now kept in Armagh Cathedral, shows a man holding the points of his horse-like ears.

Both these sculptures probably represent well-known Irish mythological figures. The first could be the king of the Tuatha Dé Danann called 'Nuadha of the Silver Arm'. Kings were expected to be physically perfect so when Nuadha lost an arm in battle he acquired a magical silver one. The figure is wearing a helmet with the stumps of two horns protruding from it.

The other statue also tells a tale of physical imperfection: Labhraidh Loingseach, a king with horse's ears, executed anyone who saw them, including his barbers. One, however, successfully pleaded for his life by promising he would never tell anyone. However, he told his secret to a tree that was cut down and carved into a harp. When played before the king it sang out 'Labhraidh Loingseach has horse's ears' after which the king was stricken with remorse and uncovered them.

IV. *Early Christianity*

Early Christianity

421. Palladius appointed bishop in Ireland.

Mid-fifth century. St Patrick.

Christianity spreads.

c.540–560. Plague arrives and eruption in far east causes two years without summers: "loss of bread".

560. The old rituals conducted at Tara for the last time.

600–900. *The age of monasteries. Many foundations started by Irish missionaries in Europe.*

c.700. Knowledge of mortar technology brought to Ireland; first stone and mortar churches built at important sites: Armagh, Clonmacnoise, Kells and Ferns the earliest recorded.

c.700–900. The great illuminated manuscripts are produced.

c.700–850. The Irish high cross developed and sculpted at many monasteries.

c.790s. Arrival of the Vikings, searching for gold and slaves.

c.900. First round towers built at important monasteries.

1167. Diarmat Mac Murchadha lands with Normans to regain his kingdom of Leinster.

IMPROVING TIMES AND ROMAN WAYS

*Part of a Bronze Age Irish gold torc inscribed
with Roman lettering found at Newgrange,
Co. Meath. The inscription, 'SCBONS.MB',
defies explanation.*

Ireland had little contact with Roman Britain until its military shield weakened in the fourth century. Then, like many other 'barbarians' on the empire's periphery, the Irish took to raiding. Eighty per cent of all the Roman coins in Ireland were found buried in the mound of Newgrange, so the tomb was still a remarkably sacred place three thousand years after it was built.

The Irish also settled the western edges of Roman Britain, on Anglesea, and in coastal areas from Pembrokeshire to Cornwall. They were apparently led by warriors of the Laigin (Leinster) dynasty in Anglesea and of the Uí Líatháin and Déisi Muman from Munster further south. They adopted the superior cattle and crops of the Romano-British as well as the La Tène implements that had already transformed British agriculture: iron spades, ploughs, sickles and scythes, as well as iron saws, chisels and axes.

The natives of west Wales also used another La Tène innovation, houses and farmyards surrounded by banked and palisaded enclosures. The settlers adopted this idea and later took it back to Ireland, where it inspired the Irish ring forts. These were the residences of a new social phenomenon: small-scale landowners with a number of dependents, who became increasingly important as the tribal system weakened.

Post-Roman and Early-Christian Sites

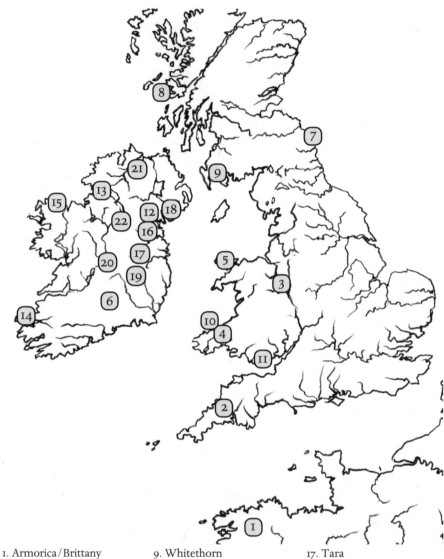

1. Armorica/Brittany
2. Tintagel
3. Wroxeter
4. Dyfed
5. Angelsea
6. Cashel
7. Lindisfarne
8. Iona

9. Whitethorn
10. St David's
11. Llancarfan
12. Armagh
13. Lough Derg
14. Dingle Peninsula
15. Foghill/Volcut
16. Slane

17. Tara
18. Saul & Downpatrick
19. Kildare
20. Clonmacnoise
21. Derry
22. Kells

One of Ireland's epic tales, the eighth-century AD *Expulsion of the Déisi* tells how their leader, Eochaid Allmuir mac Art Corb, was a high king who sailed to Britain after being expelled from Tara and that his descendants, the Déisi Muman, ruled over Demetia (Dyfed) in south Wales for several generations. In reality the Déisi Muman were a low-status group from Munster who embellished their history after rising to power.

Another consequence of these British contacts was the arrival of literacy. The two earliest examples of writing in Ireland use standard Roman lettering. One is on a fragment of a block from Station Island on Lough Derg, the island associated with St Patrick and his Purgatory in the Middle Ages, and reads '[——] OR[——] ORNECNVS ET ELISA SOMNIVM I[——]' (… Ornecnus and Elisa sleep …). It was carved with a drill, a standard late-Roman method. The other inscription is even more enigmatic. The letters 'SCBONS.MB' were incized into a piece of a Bronze Age gold torc. No sense can be made of it, but it was amongst the Roman-period offerings at Newgrange.

An ogham stone from Coolmagort, Co. Kerry.

Next came the ogham script. Irish legend says it is named after its inventor, Oghma, a brother of the Daghdha. He was also called *Grian-eces*, the sun poet, 'most knowledgeable in speech and poetry'. Ogham was in use in Ireland by the fourth century and worked on a system derived from Roman numerical tally sticks, with letters represented by differently angled sets of notches incised on either side of a straight line. The letters are grouped according to the pronunciation system of a third-century Roman grammarian – vowels in one, plosives in another and so on – clearly devised by somebody with Latin learning.

Ogham's great advantage was that inscriptions could be made without writing materials or stonemasons; many were presumably cut into wood or other perishable materials, but only one on a bone knife handle survives. The Irish in Britain made bilingual monuments as territorial markers and memorials, using Latin in Roman lettering as well as Irish in ogham, while in Ireland they are, with one exception using Viking runes, only in ogham. It looks, therefore, as though ogham was first used for stone monuments in Ireland. Most inscriptions are in counties Kerry, Cork and Waterford.

There are some ogham inscriptions in northwest Wales and southwest Britain, but most are in the area settled by the Déisi Muman in southwest Wales. One, in Castelldwyran, has a Christian cross and memorializes a person called Voteporix with the Roman title *Protictoris*. There are several stories about individuals with versions of this name. The British writer Gildas said, *c*.540 AD, that the current tyrant (ruler) of Demetia was Vortiporius, a widower grey with age, who was so wicked that he must be one of the beasts of the Apocalypse. Gildas's *Expulsion* says Vortiporius's Irish name was *Gartbuir*, and that he was a descendant of the Eochaid Allmuir (Overseas Eochaid) who brought the Muman

The citadel of Cashel, Co. Tipperary, showing the thirteenth-century cathedral and the eleventh century round tower.

Déisi to Dyfed. Elsewhere it states that Vortiporius was descended from Magnus Maximus, who declared himself Roman emperor at Segontium (Caernarfon) in north Wales in 383, invaded Gaul and ruled over much of western Europe until 388. Quite possibly, Maximus invited the Muman Déisi to settle in Wales in return for military support.

When the Déisi Muman returned to Ireland, they named their Munster citadel Cashel from *castellum*, the Latin for 'fortress'. It was one of many Roman words introduced to describe the new forms of organization, technology, beliefs and commodities that the settlers brought back to Ireland. The new ways arrived, like the Neolithic 'cultural package', with their own set of rituals, rules and religion. In this case it was Christianity.

A shaped stone from St James's Church, St Kew, Cornwall, inscribed 'IVSTI' in Latin script, and '[I]USTI' in Ogham.

A CHRISTIAN FOOTFALL

For centuries Christianity was an underground faith offering hope to the oppressed and dispossessed and frequently attacked by the authorities, but in 325 AD Constantine gave it official backing. Soon afterwards he moved to his new capital, Constantinople, and over the following decades, mainly thanks to large tax incentives, it became the faith of choice for the propertied and ruling elites.

The old religions were finally outlawed in the 390s. Christianity was now the Roman state religion, but civil war and barbarian invasions were ravaging the empire, and in 410 Alaric and his Goths sacked Rome. Just a year later, the British lost imperial support, and Roman Britain spiralled into decline. Trade and industry collapsed, towns were abandoned, and stone or brick buildings were replaced with wooden ones, but the British elite still saw themselves as Roman citizens, used Latin, and followed the new religion.

Ogham stone, Aglish, Co. Kerry. Swastikas were frequently used as decorative features in late-Roman times.

As with the earliest Neolithic contacts, Christianity first appears in the Irish southwest. The Dingle Peninsula has many standing stones engraved with early-Christian symbols carved over ogham inscriptions. These stones were turned upside down, part of the old ogham inscriptions were buried in the ground, and Christian symbols cut over other ones, a very public statement of cultural change. A good example is the Aglish pillar in Kerry. It has a Maltese cross in a circle with two swastikas and a spear carved over its ogham inscription, while the fifth-century ecclesiastical enclosure of Reask, also in Kerry, has two more. One has a Maltese cross flanked by peacocks set inside a square, while the other has a cross inside a circle surrounded by swirling La Tène decoration, for the carvers knew few Christian symbols. Another, at Kilfountain in County Kerry, has a stone basin at its feet like those in megalithic tombs.

Ogham stone from Kilfountain, Co. Kerry. In the early-Christian period, ogham stones were frequently turned upside down and over-carved with Christian symbols.

PATRICK

Ireland's first historical figure, Patrick, belongs to this period. He was from a Romano-British gentry family whose *villula* was either in southwest Britain or near Banna, a Hadrian's Wall fort east of Carlisle.[54] He spoke Latin as well as the local Celtic tongue, and aged sixteen was seized by Irish raiders. He was then sold into slavery in Ireland. Many years later, as a bishop, he wrote two documents that are Ireland's earliest literary works and indeed the only surviving fifth-century documents from the British Isles. They were his response to attacks made against him by Romano-British opponents.

Slave collar from Lagore crannog, Co. Meath. Patrick writes about being put in chains by his opponents on occasion.

Patrick says he was a slave in Ireland for seven years, looking after his owner's herds close to 'the wood of Voclut [*Silva Vocluti*] … near the western sea'. Scholars have agonized over Voclut, as this is the only Irish place named by Patrick, but very possibly it was Patrick's rendering of the old Irish word for 'northern', *fochla*, and that he lived near a large wood or forest in the northern parts of Ireland. The 'western sea' would then simply be the sea to the west of Britain, the Irish Sea, and the traditions identifying his place of captivity as north Antrim could be correct.

The earliest source for this tradition are two *Lives* of Patrick composed *c.*670. They both stated that his slave master was Milliuc, the king and chief druid of the Braid Valley kingdom. This was a stretch of land running northeast from the area around the present town of Ballymena, with the mountain of Slemish, where Patrick supposedly looked after Milliuc's herds, at its core. At the time it was one of about 150 tiny Irish kingdoms,[55] and those that adopted the new ways early on were usually at some distance from the tribal centres. As at Armagh, churches were built on old ritual sites or hills near local royal sites. It was a forceful statement by local rulers of their support for the new ways.

There was a rift within the new official faith. In the early fifth century, the papacy was battling Pelagianism, the teachings of a British divine who maintained that every believer was liberated by his personal relationship with God. Christianity was useless as a Roman imperial tool if it did not support the dictates of central authority, so the papacy declared Pelagianism a heresy and took St Augustine's position that salvation depended on obeying the rules of the Church. The papacy sent two missions in the 420s to root out Pelagianism in Britain and soon after the second, in 431 AD, the pope sent a member of the team, Palladius, as bishop to the Christians in Ireland. The purpose must have been to eliminate Pelagianism there too. It is hardly surprising that it was followed in Ireland, as the first Irish Christian communities came from Britain, and semi-Pelagian views were still §expressed in Ireland a century later.

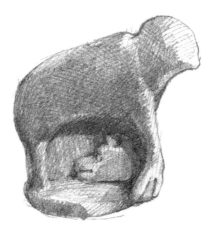

Carving of a 'bear' with a wolf's head between its legs from Armagh Cathedral. Three of these pre-Christian 'bears' were kept in the Cathedral but one has been stolen. They might relate to the pagan ritual site that was here before it was given to the Christian community.

Patrick's career must have overlapped with Palladius's time but his texts give no dates. After seven years of slavery he says he escaped, journeying two hundred miles across Ireland to a place where he found a boat that was about to head overseas. After some hesitation its crew invited him along. Probably they wanted to offer their services as mercenaries, and a Christian Roman-Briton would have been a useful interpreter and go-between.

Some Irish mercenaries did well in Britain, as its communities struggled without the protection of the legions. The first king of Gwynnedd was an Irish warrior and a reused fragment of a tombstone in Wroxeter, Shropshire, the fourth-largest town of Roman Britain, has an Irish inscription on it: 'CUNORIX MACUSMA QUICOLINE', 'Hound-king, son of the Holly tribe'. Cunorix was presumably an Irish petty king, the leader of an Irish mercenary band defending the city. It was a potentially profitable occupation: two hoards of silver bars and cut-up silver pieces have turned up in Ireland. It was a standard method of paying soldiers after the currency failed.

Wroxeter memorial inscription to 'CUNORIX MACUSMA QUICOLINE' ('Hound-king, son of the Holly tribe'). Cunorix was presumably an Irish petty king, whose men were employed here as mercenaries for this sub-Roman town's protection.

Patrick became a priest and returned to his parents. To their dismay, he then declared he intended to return to Ireland. He must have been made a bishop by British Church authorities, presumably to minister to Ireland's Christian communities, but Patrick had other ideas. He believed God had chosen him to bring Christianity to the pagan Irish, and describes several visionary experiences, hallucinations brought on by extreme stress, which he believed were messages from God.

THE IRISH MISSION

The main centre for Patrick's operations appears to have been northeast Ulster. His first success seems to have been with a petty chief in County Down, who gave him a building to use as a church. Its name, Saul or *Sabhall*, is a Hibernicized version of *stabellum*, the Latin for 'barn'. A tradition in the *Lives* of 670 AD said that Patrick cursed some people for building a rath on a Sunday and shouted 'Mudebroth' at them. The phrase was incomprehensible to the locals, but a storm that night made the rath collapse so the phrase was remembered. 'Mudebroth' could be a version of a British Celtic phrase meaning 'by God's judgment', and if so, these are Patrick's only recorded words in his mother tongue.

Patrick's activities frequently got him into dangerous situations. He paid the sons of friendly kings to escort him into difficult areas, but was imprisoned several times. He claimed, however, to have had success, and the *c.*670 *Lives* talk of him establishing a church at Armagh. The discovery of some possibly fifth-century Christian graves at Armagh suggests a very early-Christian community, and implies the support of the local king, for Armagh and Navan were the Uladh kingdom's ritual sites. Soon after Patrick's time the Uí Néills drove the Uladh kings out of the Armagh region, so local tales were embroidered to suit the new rulers and this probably accounts for the curious mixture of magic, wonder-working and mythological confrontations in the stories about Patrick at Armagh.

A similar group of wonder tales of *c.*670 describe confrontations with the old pagan headquarters at Tara. These say that after Patrick demonstrated that his magical powers were greater than those of the druids, the king of Tara gave him Slane, an old ritual hill fifteen kilometres to the northeast, for his church. This suggests that a Christian presence was only tolerated at this kingdom's periphery. The old pagan customs continued to operate at Tara for many years more, and in the tales the king did not embrace the new faith. The Uí Néills, in fact, also conquered Tara and the Meath kingdom soon after Patrick's time, so these tales were probably embroidered for their benefit.

The British Church authorities, however, tried hard to stop Patrick, and he wrote two documents in response. The longer document, his 'Confession', is a defence against specific accusations. One was that as a youth, before his capture by Irish pirates, he committed a serious sin (possibly an initiation into one of the old Roman cults, which were still popular, if illegal). He also said he was accused of spreading blasphemies (heresies), misappropriating Church funds and having 'pagan leanings'.

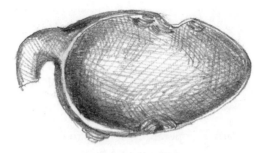

This jet spoon is of a type used in early-Christian ceremonies. It is one of the few Roman-style objects in Ireland that might date from Patrick's time and have a Christian context. Jet had been regarded as having magical qualities since Neolithic times.

Patrick must have had influential supporters, for the attempt failed. However, when he won an Irish tribe over to Christianity his British opponents resorted to violence. The tribe, probably a Scoti tribe in north Antrim, had come together at the tribal capital to be received into the Church. The day after their induction into the Christian life, when the participants were still in their ceremonial white garments and had sacramental oil smeared on their foreheads, the soldiers of a Romano-British leader called Coroticus appeared. They killed many, took the rest prisoner and looted and burnt the houses. Then they divided the women amongst themselves and transported the men to Scotland, where they were sold as slaves to pagan Picts.

The murder, rape and enslavement of a large group of Irish converts by an army detachment commanded by a Romano-British Christian is astonishing by any standards. The most plausible explanation is that Coroticus believed Patrick was teaching heresies, presumably Pelagian teachings, and that as a Roman citizen he felt he had a duty to stamp them out. Patrick's defence was to detail how God had commanded him to convert the Irish in a series of visions. He never suggests he had Church authorization for his missionary work, so his defence sounds remarkably Pelagian, but he used his authority as a bishop to excommunicate Coroticus and his men for their crimes against fellow Christians.

CONVERTING THE IRISH

One of several bells purported to have belonged to St Patrick. All were, in fact, made long after his time, but seventh- and eighth-century accounts of his life claimed he gave a bell to each church he founded.

Many early Christians, including Patrick, believed that the Second Coming would happen once Christ's words had been heard everywhere, so his missionary work had an urgent purpose. Ireland's new landed class also had a pressing need to justify its rise at the expense of tribal authority, and Christianity proved extremely useful. Each little kingdom could now have a bishop's diocese covering its territory, to give it further cohesion.

Patrick describes his male and female converts taking vows of celibacy and devoting themselves to God, becoming either hermits or celibate members in a household. It was a normal religious expression at the time, but one of Patrick's disciples, Mochtu, established a monastery at Louth, the first in Ireland. In Ireland, as in mainland Europe, monasteries acted as landowners, encouraging the spread of iron tools, better land use and improved agriculture. Most churches were small, more shrines than places for large congregations, and like the first stone crosses the few precious objects produced in this early period, such as tiny transportable reliquaries, were mainly decorated with La Tène patterns.

An early-seventh-century reliquary from Clonmore, Co. Armagh. It is only 8cm long and was designed to be worn around the neck. A few European relics had reached Ireland by this time and a number associated with early-Irish saints were also venerated.

Gallarus Oratory, Dingle Peninsula, Co. Kerry. It is variously dated from the sixth to the twelfth centuries, but is in any case a fine example of a stone church built without mortar. Its interior measures approximately 4.8m x 3m, and is lit by a tiny round-headed window in the east wall.

THE RISE OF THE UÍ NÉILLS

The Liath Fáil, Stone of Destiny, Tara, Co. Meath. This undecorated, phallic stone is supposed to have been used in inauguration rites performed by the new king at Tara.

Ireland's tribal structure was modified many times over the millennia, and in the early-Christian era was reshaped once again. Powerful dynasties amalgamated large territories under their personal rule, and lorded it over the petty kings. One particular figure, Nél, had an enduring impact. He is better known as Niall Noígíallach, Niall of the Nine Hostages, and seems to have been king of Tara in the early fifth century. His epithet probably referred to hostages held from the nine 'septs'[56] of the Airghialla, a tribe living to the north of his territory, though later legends turned them into representatives from the country's five provinces and four neighbouring nations. He probably died in the 450s.

Niall came from a dynasty called the Connachta, which claimed descent from a semi-mythical figure, Conn Cétchathach, Conn of the Hundred Battles. Niall's father was said to be Eochu Muighmheadhon, 'Eochu lord of the slaves', who captured a young woman with the Roman name Carina (Cairenn in Irish) on a raid into Britain. Niall, their son, was reputed to have led more raiding expeditions into Britain, and even to have captured Patrick.

There are vivid accounts of the inauguration rituals that determined who should become king after Eochu's death. Niall and his brothers were set to work in a forge, which was then set on fire, so they had to save the smithy's implements. Niall emerged with the heaviest, the anvil, and was proclaimed the greatest. Out hunting, they met an old hag at a well who said she would give a drink to whoever would kiss her. Niall obliged, upon which she turned into a beautiful girl and announced she was the personification of sovereignty. She told him only to give his brothers a drink if they agreed that their weapons should always be placed lower than his own at their father's court. The chief druid proclaimed that Niall and his descendants would have dominion over Ireland.

The shadowy events of Niall's reign are further obscured by the introduction of three fictional cousins, the three Collas, into the narrative. The deeds ascribed to them were probably performed by Niall and his sons, including the capture of Navan and Armagh from the Uladh. The seventh-century tales about Patrick make him a contemporary of Niall's son and his successor, Loegaire, which would date them after 450, and describe dramatic confrontations with the pagan powers at Tara. Although these are heavily embellished they may be based on actual events.

Patrick is said to have lit his paschal fire just when Loegaire was lighting the spring equinox fire at Tara, to his fury. Niall attacked Patrick and his followers, so Patrick asked God to bring darkness and earthquakes down upon them. After this, Patrick and the druids competed to see who had the stronger powers. When one druid derided Christianity, Patrick had him lifted into the air and dropped so his skull was smashed on a stone. Another seventh-century account says the druid came down 'frozen solid with hail and snow mixed with sparks of fire', and that the stone containing the frozen druid is still at Tara. This must refer to a quartzite stone there, an important feature of many megalithic sites. Next, the druids brought down snow, which Patrick melted, and a fog, which he dispersed. As a final test, a Christian boy and a druid were put into a house that was then set on fire; the boy's prayers saved him, while the druid burned.

Loegaire declared that his people could become Christians if they wanted to, but stuck to the old faith himself, the typical response of a native headman confronted by missionaries and their inducements. Patrick is also said to have built a large church at Donaghmore, even further away from Tara than Slane. This suggests that Patrick's support was from lesser men in the kingdom and although Christian ways were now tolerated, the old beliefs continued. It may be relevant that a limestone pillar covered in La Tène designs at Mullaghmast in Kildare was probably carved in this period, perhaps as a public affirmation of the old beliefs. The carving was never finished.

Many subsequently claimed descent from Niall, so the name Uí Néill was born, and ultimately anglicized as O'Neill. Such genealogical claims were questionable, but the learned class was adept at tweaking. They also would find ingenious ways to relate their clients to Patrick. He was given a sister called Lupita with a flock of children by three Irish saints, and they were incorporated into the family trees.

Many of the emerging families remained powerful players for over a thousand years, including the O'Briens, the O'Connors, the O'Donnells and the Eóganacht of Munster. The uneasy symbiosis between Christianity and the old beliefs led to churches clustering around the old cult centres like Uisneach in County Westmeath, where herds of cattle were driven between two enormous fires at Bealtaine, the festival that ushered in the summer. Uisneach was Ireland's navel. Twelve rivers were said to flow from it, and Ériu, the country's goddess, lived under an outcrop called Ail na Mirenn, the Rock of the Portions, from which radiated the five-part division of Ireland. Giraldus Cambrensis also said that Stonehenge stood at Uisneach before being magically transported to Britain by Merlin.

Carved stone from Mullaghmast, Co. Kildare. This was an important prehistoric hilltop site. Many Iron Age artefacts have been found here and there are several other standing stones. In nearby Gleann Treithim the smith god Goibniu was said to have had his forge.

BRIGHID

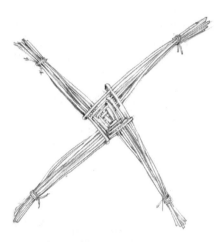

A St Bridget's Cross, traditionally made from green rushes on the first of February and thus emblematic of the countryside's reawakening after the darkest days of winter.

All over Ireland there were places with mystical associations, and as Christianity spread it adapted itself to these beliefs. An outstanding example of this is the story of St Brighid. In the late fifth or early sixth century she was a druidess presiding over Cill Dara (Kildare), a sanctuary in an oak grove dedicated to the goddess Brighid, but seeing how the wind was blowing, she converted to Christianity, turned the sanctuary into Ireland's first convent and became its abbess.

In the early seventh century, a petty king seized power in Leinster. His wife came from Brighid's sept, the Fotharta, and her brother was bishop of Kildare, so they promoted Brighid in earnest. Inevitably she gained many attributes of the goddess along the way, including power over the fertility of women and animals, and the weather. The St Brighid stories often reflect these beliefs. As a baby she was suckled by a red-eared white cow, an ancient British magical breed, and as a child working on her father's farm produced miraculous amounts of butter, milk and bacon. There are many St Brighid wells that make barren women fertile, and the perpetual fire in her Kildare church was probably a survival from the old sanctuary. Her holy day, the first of February, is Oímelg, 'Lactation', the start of pagan spring. On that day, Brighid gives milk and fertility to cows and ewes, and her devotees weave green rushes into sacred shapes.[57]

VOLCANOES AND THE PLAGUE

Ireland's line of communication with the outside world was once more via tin-rich Cornwall, now a Romano-British refuge as the Anglo-Saxons advanced. As a result, a scatter of imported objects are found across Ireland: pieces of amphorae, pots and dishes from north Africa and Greece, and a few Frankish swords. In return for Cornish tin the traders brought these things as well as communion wine. It was a small-scale version of the old Atlantic Fringe network.

Frankish sword. Although inferior to La Tène swords, these were produced in large numbers and so allowed a whole band of warriors to be equipped with effective iron swords.

In the mid-sixth century, two natural catastrophes struck. In 535 AD, a large volcanic eruption near Java and Sumatra threw quantities of dust into the atmosphere. Contemporary accounts say there were no summers for two years, and although it was not on a level with earlier events, there were severe consequences. Agriculture collapsed and starvation stalked the world. The Irish annals record a *'perditio panis'*, a loss of bread.

A greater disaster followed. The Byzantine love of ivory opened up trade with Africa via the Red Sea, bringing central-African rats to the ports. Some brought with them a new disease, the bubonic plague, reaching Egypt on the trading boats and spreading the disease around the Mediterranean. About 80 per cent of the Roman Empire's hundred million people died. The plague finally reached Ireland in 540, where it was called the *Blefed*. In 547 it returned to Britain, after which Tintagel and the other sub-Roman settlements of the West Country and Cornwall were abandoned and the 'residue of the nation' fled to Armorica[58] and Ireland. The following year a new Irish king went through the old inauguration ceremonies at Tara, but the plague returned in 550 and 553, after which Tara's rites were abandoned.

RECOVERY

Life in an early-Irish monastery.

Plagues and deadly diseases recurred frequently over the following centuries: bubonic plague, smallpox, leprosy and others known only by Irish names. They were the grim results of contacts with mainland Europe, but at least Ireland was spared the barbarian invasions that overwhelmed Roman Europe.

The worst-hit plague areas in Ireland were the thickly settled lands of the east and south, enabling people from the western peripheries rise to power. Their dialect was the first recorded form of the Irish language, and their power base was the new class of small landowners who lived in ring forts surrounded by tenants and adherents. They were the subjects of petty kings, who were themselves subordinate to emerging dynasties like the Uí Néills and Uí Briúins. This was a world defined by kinships, obligations and the Church. All had long memories of who had done what to whom and these were woven into poems and stories.

There was further expansion. The Scoti of Dalriada in north Ulster moved across the sea into the lands and islands of Argyll, and, for a century and a half, Irish kings ruled this realm before it split into Irish and Scottish halves. These settlers brought their Irish culture and language, and ultimately gave their name to the whole country.

There were no towns or castles in this world, only ring forts, hill forts and fortified islands. The monasteries now emerged as centres of a higher culture, and, like so much else, the inspiration came from sub-Roman Britain. The first recorded incomer after Patrick and Mochtu's time was Finnian, who came from St Cadoc's abbey of Llancarfan *c.*500 to found Clonard in Meath. There he taught three monastic founders: Brendan, who set up Clonfert; Ciarán, the founder of Clonmacnoise; and Colum Cille of Durrow, Derry and Iona. Another divine, Enda, came from Whithorn in Galloway, the religious hub of the British kingdom of Strathclyde, and King Aenghus of Cashel granted him Inishmore in the Aran Islands.

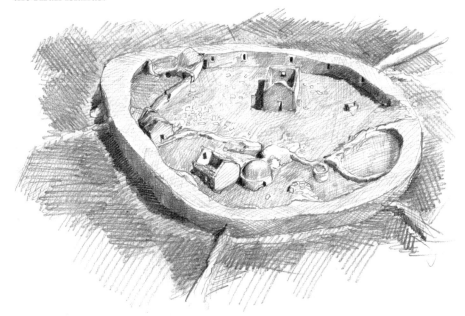

Early monastic settlement, Inishmurray, Co. Sligo. St Molaise came from Whithorn to found a monastery here in the sixth century. The round stone house in the enclosure is called Teach na Teine, *the House of Fire. If all fires on the island went out, a piece of turf laid on a stone in this house would miraculously catch fire. The establishment was despoiled by the Vikings in 807.*

From their inception in Egypt, monasteries were enclosed by rectangular, walled precincts. This shape was adopted by the earliest Irish monasteries, such as Clonmacnoise, but they soon turned to the rounder form used for raths and royal sites. Inside, these precincts were divided into zones for cells and domestic activities, while at the centre were the church and graveyard.

These monasteries were creative power houses. They kept libraries and preserved Latin and Greek literature when learning was vanishing elsewhere in western Europe. The monks also began writing textual commentaries in Irish. Having created a means of writing the vernacular, they committed the epics, tales and poetry of their own people to writing. It was the first European litera-ture other than Latin or Greek, and included some remarkable nature poetry:

Scél lem dúib	A story for you:
dordaid dam	stag roars
snigid gaim	winter falls
ro faith sam	summer's gone
Gáith ard úar	Cold high wind
ísel grían	sun low
gair a rrith	short its run
ruirthech rían	seas run strong
rorúad rath	Deep red ferns,
ro cleth cruth	their shape gone,
ro gab gnáth	barnacle geese
giugrann guth	call with a cry
Ro gab úacht	Cold holds
etti én	birds' wings
aigre ré	icy times:
é mo scél.	That's my tale.[59]

As the monasteries helped local dynasties increase their power, they turned them into family enterprises, with married abbots and tenant farmers who inherited monastic functions. However, the monks introduced many technological improvements, including better farming equipment and water mills. These replaced hand mills, and were often built near ring forts as well as monasteries. The control of milling was a way of maintaining power over the population and the monasteries became so powerful that they even waged private wars.

The Irish vision was not only focussed on Rome and the Holy Land, but also, like Patrick, on places where God's Word was unknown. Colum Cille's monastery on Iona was thus founded to bring Christianity to Scotland, essentially a political move to open up more channels of influence for Colum Cille's family, the northern Uí Néill.

Centuries later, a morality tale was invented. Colum Cille, it was said, only moved to Iona after a fearsome dispute. He had borrowed a Gospel book from Finnian of Moville, copied it without permission, returned the original and kept his copy. Finnian was furious, and when the high king at Tara, Diarmad mac Cearrbheoil, was asked for his verdict he said, 'To every cow her calf, to every book its copy.' It was the first copyright ruling. The northern Uí Néill then waged war against Tara, King Diarmad died in battle and Colum Cille was exiled.

Although the tale is fictional, Colum Cille's success was real, and Irish monks were soon much in demand. Aidan left Iona to found Lindisfarne monastery for the king of Northumbria; Fursa went from Munster to East Anglia to build one for King Sigbert in a ruined Roman fort before starting several more in Gaul for Clovis, the Frankish king. Another monk, Columbanus, sailed from Bangor to Gaul and founded monasteries in the Vosges before setting up Bobbio in Italy, where he died in 635.[60]

These men all came from Irish royal families, and could present themselves at other courts with assurance. Dozens of Irish houses were created across western Europe and this impetus only waned as the papacy reasserted itself in the late seventh century. This was the background to the confrontation at Whitby in 664, when the Irish monks of Lindisfarne debated with papal representatives the proper way to calculate Easter, and lost. By the end of that century, all Irish institutions had accepted the new Easter dating system.

A warrior engraved on one of the two pillars on either side of the high cross at Carndonagh, on the Inishowen Peninsula, Co. Donegal. It probably dates from the seventh century.

CHURCH ART

Ireland's creativity reached a zenith between 650 and 1000 AD. The vigour and originality of the artistic works are astonishing. Thanks to Ireland's isolation, only a limited number of images or manuscripts ever reached here, but these were enthusiastically adopted. Many of the best illuminated manuscripts were, in fact, produced by the Irish diaspora, particularly in Iona and Northumbria, where there was more contact with the outside world. As a result, Anglo-Saxon, Frankish, Roman and Scandinavian elements entered into the mix and inter-twined with the Byzantine, Syrian and Coptic elements that came via southern routes. Irish imagery therefore followed formulae from earlier Christian manu-scripts; the idea for carpet-page illuminations came from Syria; and Irish 'inter-lace' has Anglo-Saxon, Scandinavian and Middle Eastern roots. Only one scrap survives from any of the Middle Eastern manuscripts that came here, a blank piece of Egyptian papyrus embedded in the binding of the eighth-century Faddan Mór Psalter.

The style of illumination developed in the British Isles during this period is called 'Hiberno-Saxon' or 'Insular'. The most outstanding work, the Lindisfarne Gospels, was made at the end of the seventh century in Northumbria, either for St Cuthbert before he died in 687, or to commemorate his elevation to sainthood in 698. The similarity of its illuminations to those in other works like the Book of Kells shows how interconnected this society was. Books went from one place to another as monks moved, and ideas and images spread. St Cuthbert, meanwhile, devoted his energy to melding Irish–Ionian customs with those of Europe.

The Irish were eager for any information about the Holy Land. When Arculph, a Gaulish pilgrim, was stranded on Iona on his way home, he paid for his board and lodging by making a manuscript describing the most important sites, thus creating the most detailed Holy Land guide before the arrival of Islam.

Many of the diaspora's best manuscripts came to Ireland after the Viking raids began. The Book of Kells, for example, acquired its name because the Kells monastery became its refuge after the Iona monks left it there, along with St Columba's shrine and the Book of Durrow. Until then, it was called St Colum-ba's *Soscela mór*, his Great Gospel Book, and was probably created on Iona. Many metalwork masterpieces also only exist because they were hidden away. The Tara Brooch turned up in a County Meath field in 1850 and the Ardagh Chalice, a masterpiece of early-Christian metalwork, in a stone-lined cist in Kerry when some ground was dug for potatoes in 1868.

Ardagh Chalice, c.800 AD, was found amongst a hoard at Reerasta Rath near Ardagh, Co. Limerick. It was deposited c.900 and consisted of the chalice, a copper-alloy plain-stemmed cup and four brooches.

Another remarkable achievement were the stone high crosses, the largest sculptures of eighth-century western Europe. Admittedly the early-Christian Irish communities had continued the pagan tradition of venerating standing stones, but carved the new religion's symbols onto them. The high crosses, however, were a new departure, inspired by descriptions of the Jewelled Cross in Jerusalem. This jewel-encrusted wooden cross was erected in the fifth century by the Emperor Theodosius inside the Church of the Holy Sepulchre, where Constantine's mother, St Helena, had identified the site of the Crucifixion, Christ's tomb and the True Cross.

The cross only became a Christian symbol when Constantine's successors started using a cross encircled by a victor's wreath as their emblem. It commemorated the Battle of the Milvian Bridge of 312 AD, when Constantine defeated Maxentius and became sole emperor of the empire's western half, a victory

Early-Christian-period Roman sarcophagus with angels supporting a version of Constantine's emblem: a victor's wreath surrounding a cross.

attributed to a vision in which God told Constantine to have crosses daubed on his men's shields. It became known as the moment when God's intervention caused the Christianization of the Roman Empire.

The earliest Irish high crosses are topped with round objects representing the domed shape of the Church of the Holy Sepulchre. They were thus memorials to the holiest objects and places in Palestine as well as St Helena's discoveries and Constantine's conversion. The earliest are found in Northumbria beside churches founded by the Irish; however, the imagery on them resembles late-Roman or Pictish figurative relief sculpture, while the early-Irish high crosses are a riot of abstract designs.

One of the three ninth-century high crosses at Kilkieran, Co. Kilkenny. There are two similar high crosses at Ahenny, Co. Tipperary.

The early stone crosses imitate earlier wooden ones. A few wooden fragments survive in Ireland, along with some embossed metal plaques, probably imitating the form of the Jewelled Cross. From the tenth century, the Irish followed the Northumbrian formula of carving Old and New Testament scenes, with the Crucifixion and the Last Judgment used as central images. Pilgrimage routes led to the monasteries where the crosses stood, so the Irish could experience something of the sacred land that few would ever reach. Monumental stone crosses were also produced at the other end of Europe, in Armenia and Georgia, between the fifth and seventh centuries. These, too, were inspired by Theodosius's Jewelled Cross and often incorporated the Constantinian device. As many refugees from the region came to western Europe after the Islamic conquests of the seventh and eighth centuries, they could well have brought the concept of the high cross with them.

There was another source of inspiration: the Visigoths of southern Spain in the seventh century engraved their grave slabs with ringed crosses identical to the Irish ones. This form came from Coptic Egypt, where the Constantinian device had melded with the 'ankh' sign for eternity to create a cross with a victor's wreath at its centre. It seems, therefore, that the idea of putting a circle round the crosses came from Coptic Egypt via Visigothic Spain, but the idea behind the high cross not only originated in Jerusalem but was possibly also influenced by descriptions of those erected in Armenia and Georgia.

Detail from a late-fourth-century Roman sarcophagus.

Ireland and Myth

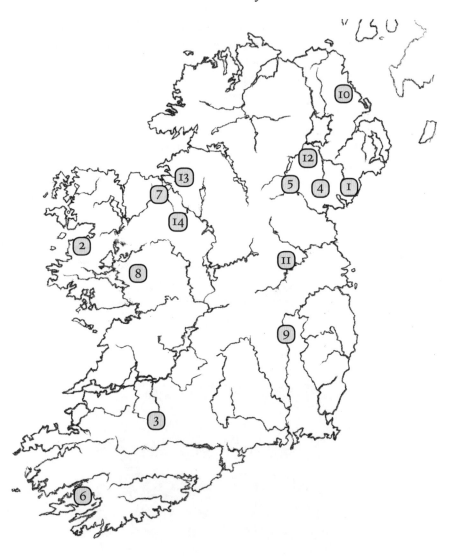

1. Slieve Donard
2. Croagh Patrick
3. Knockainey
4. Slieve Gullion
5. Altadeven Wood & St Patrick's Chair
6. Beara Peninsula
7. Knockanshee

8. Knockma
9. Kildare
10. Slemish
11. Tara
12. Armagh & Navan
13. Knocknarea
14. Crúachan

HOLY HILLS

Although the old faiths officially lost out to the new religion, beliefs or customs did not change, though many of the gods and spirits were given a Christian twist. Patrick was said to have set seven watchers inside important hills to keep Ireland safe until the Second Coming, one of which was Slieve Donard, the highest of the Mournes. Donard, the baptized son of the last pagan king of Mourne, lives in it. The megalithic passage grave on its summit is his chapel. At midsummer a pilgrimage was made to the mountain top, and a Mass was said in the tomb.

Portal tomb and Slieve Donard, Co. Down.

In most places, the old myths and beliefs were left unadulterated. Knockainey, or Cnoc Áine, in County Limerick, for example, was still the home of Áine, the local sovereignty goddess. People who climbed it the night before a major festival might be taken down into her realms, while on Midsummer Eve the local farmers carried burning brands to its top, walked clockwise round its three megalithic barrows and then ran back to their fields to walk the brands round them, ensuring their fertility.

This hill was one of three in the county that were *sídh*, dwellings of the otherworld. Cnoc Gráinne was inhabited by the sun goddess and the third, Cnoc Fírinne, the Hill of Truth, housed the king of the otherworld spirits, the *Sí*. He was a god of death and fertility and new stones were added to his cairn by those climbing it, while unmarried women left gifts on the hillside at Bealtaine and Samhain, as well as flowers on its summit at Lughnasa, to ensure a good future.

Even that most Christian-seeming mountain, Croagh Patrick, has a pagan past. Patrick battled against his fiercest supernatural opponents. The annual pilgrimage to its summit in honour of Ireland's patron saint happens on the Sunday nearest Lughnasa, so the old beliefs determine even this event. In any case, the mountain had had great power for thousands of years before Patrick, as much of Ireland's prehistoric gold was mined around it.

St Patrick's Chair in Altadeven Wood, Co. Armagh.
Near this 2m-high stone block is the saint's holy
'well', a rock with a water-filled 25cm depression,
which is said never to run dry.

The old gods also acquired new identities. St Brighid was amalgamated with her goddess namesake and Crom Dubh became the name given to all old male gods. This epithet meant the 'dark croucher', the Devil, but it allowed old beliefs to continue, for Patrick was said to have converted Crom Dubh at the end of a long struggle, rendering him religiously acceptable. A ninth-century story said that Patrick destroyed a stone idol called Cenn Cruaich that stood surrounded by twelve lesser gods on a plain in Cavan, which then sank into the ground. This sounds like the destruction of a stone circle, but as Cenn Cruaich means 'hard head' it might refer to a stone head. There are also 'holy wells', including one beside St Patrick's Chair at Altadeven, which are simply carved depressions in rocks. Stories are told about how they never run dry and that the water has healing or life-giving properties. These 'wells' and the tales attached to them originated in the world of Bronze Age cup-and-ring rock carvings, which were probably also involved with ritual use of water.[61]

A similar process happened to female divinities. Local names were often replaced by that of the Cailleach Bhéarra, a sovereignty goddess from the Beara Peninsula in Cork/Kerry, who changed from old hag to fair maiden at a kiss. However, Knocknashee in Sligo continued to be the Hill of the Fairies, and Maedhbh, the intoxicating war goddess, lives in her megalithic cairn on Knockma in Galway, with Finnbheara, the fairies' leader, in another. Maedhbh is said to stand inside hers with her men, spear in hand, waiting for the moment to attack Ulster, while the father-sun god, the Daghdha, inhabits a hilltop megalithic tomb nearby.

The popular ninth-century story, *Buile Suibhne*, The Tale of the Mad Sweeney, vividly depicts tensions between the pagan and Christian worlds. Suibhne, a fictitious king of Dál nAraidhe in northeast Ulster, opposed the arrival of Christianity, threw the psalter of one priest who tried to build a church in his territory into a lake and killed another who sprinkled him with holy water. He went insane from the curse of a saint and wandered through Ireland, kept alive by lapping milk from a dent in a cowpat. He heard about the death of his family and returned twice to his kingdom, but each time left again, madder than ever and rejected by his wife for another man. In the end, the jealous husband of a woman who fed him scraps of food ran him through with a spear. Mortally wounded, he confessed his sins to St Moling, and died at his church door. The tale was inspired by the British tale of Lailoken who went mad after seeing demons in the sky during the fatal British defeat at Arfderydd in 574 (as did Merlin). Suibhne's sobriquet, *geilt*, is the Old Welsh *gwyllt*, 'wild'. The word is also used to describe the valley he lived in for a year with another deranged king: Gleann na nGeallt, the Glen of the Madmen.

Teampal Bheanáin, Inishmore, Aran Islands. An eleventh-century church dedicated to St Benignus, one of St Patrick's disciples.

GODS, SAINTS AND FESTIVALS

A Sheela na Gig from Rahara churchyard, Co. Roscommon. Sheelas are frequently grimacing with the pain of childbirth and were invoked by women seeking protection in their hour of need.

Lugh's harvest festival, Lughnasa, continued to be celebrated all over Ireland. People congregated for games and contests, drinking, matchmaking and dancing; sometimes the proceedings were linked to a Christian holy day. Bealtaine marked the onset of summer, when cattle were driven between bonfires or dunked in loughs or rivers, and Samhain, the ancestor festival, marked the onset of winter, a break in time when otherworld forces and spirits could slip into our world. This powerful concept was half-Christianized as Halloween. Midwinter rites were attached to Christmas, and St Patrick's Day was conveniently close to the spring equinox, when life is reborn. This was celebrated by eating wood sorrel, the first edible plant to appear in the woods, and therefore seen as life-giving. As wood sorrel is a trefoil and Celtic mythology placed such significance upon divinities with triple natures, the plant had mystical significance, entering Irish Christian lore as the shamrock used by Patrick to teach the concept of the

Trinity. Wood sorrel continued to be collected and eaten, but as the old woods where the sorrel grew were cut down and clover was introduced for cattle, this inedible trefoil was called shamrock and wood sorrel's symbolism as the food of rebirth was lost.

In folklore, Patrick had a wife called Sheela na Gig, who protected women giving birth. Carved images of her were venerated, and built into churches, to the disgust of the priests as she is depicted full frontal and naked, legs apart and opening her birth passage with her hands. She was, in fact, a Norman introduction to the mythological mix rather than an older Irish tradition (Sheela was the Irish version of the Norman St Cecilia) and their castles often have carvings of Sheelas on their outer walls.[62]

A bullán or 'cursing stone' from Co. Fermanagh.

Many ancient sacred wells were transferred to other saints than Brighid. Each had specific properties, such as healing arthritic joints or rheumy eyes, from stopping toothache to curing insanity (thanks to the lithium in some springs) and often there are *bulláns* beside them, rocks with round dips in their surface into which stones are ground for curses and blessings. These 'cursing stones' are turned one way or the other to invoke good or evil, a magical turning of stone on stone in use since megalithic times, as the round dips ground into many incised stones reveal.

During the Christianization of the old mythological themes, the Irish saints became wonder-working magicians who flew through the air, confined monsters to lakes, cured diseases and killed with curses. The tales about Patrick circulating in seventh-century Armagh describe just such a series of magical events: the local chief, who is a personification of the Celtic god, the Daghdha, opposed Patrick, but he demonstrated his power by killing the Daghdha's stallion with a curse and then bringing it back to life. Eventually he conceded defeat, gave Patrick his great cauldron (such cauldrons never ran out of food, so this was a magical promise of constant plenty), and his ritual hill. Some pagan stone carvings were kept here, as proof of Patrick's deeds.

These tales were important because they explained why the old spirit powers gave way to Patrick in terms that made sense to a semi-pagan audience. Many of the legends about sacred hills were also given a Christian twist, although the altered stories always accepted that the old spirits were powerful. Ireland thus made this transition without shedding old beliefs. The monasteries now became the goals of pilgrimage, large crowds gathered at them for feast days and the scenes carved on the high crosses explained the Bible stories.

Horse and rider from Banagher Cross, Co. Offaly.

VIKINGS

Norse graffiti of a ship on a plank found in the Viking settlement at Wood Quay, Dublin.

Viking raids began in the 790s. They hit Britain's east coast first, but on their return in 794 went west to find the monasteries on Iona and Rathlin. Tory was plundered next, followed by Inishmuray, Inishbofin and Skellig Michael. The raiders returned each year, gradually moving inland, first to places near the sea like Derry, Bangor or Cork, then up rivers to Clonmacnoise, Devenish and Slane and finally to landlocked places like Armagh.

Ironically, much of the impetus came from Charlemagne's attempt to recreate the Roman Empire. His currency reform of 793–4 led to a big demand for gold and silver. As Islam now dominated the Middle East and the Mediterranean, Charlemagne looked north for precious metals and the Vikings became his suppliers. They also wanted young females to sell to Islamic tribes on the Volga in exchange for Silk Route luxuries for Charlemagne's court.

After Charlemagne's death this trade collapsed, so the Vikings took to colonizing. In the 840s they founded a *longphort*, a protected landing place, at Dublin followed by others at Waterford, Wexford, Cork and Limerick. These, Ireland's first towns, had a strong Irish flavour. The houses looked like standard rectangular Viking houses, but the walls were made of woven withies not wooden beams, as the Irish workmen used their roundhouse building methods.

When the Vikings reached Iceland in the 860s, they found Irish monks already living there. According to Dicuil, an Irish monk who wrote his geographical book *De mensura Orbis terrae* in 825, they had been using Iceland as a summer retreat for about a hundred years.

> It is now thirty years since clerics, who live on the island from the first of February to the first of August, told me that not only at the summer solstice, but in the days round about it, the setting sun hides itself as though behind a small hill in such a way that there was no darkness at all there save for a very short space of time.
>
> (Translated by J.J Tierney)

The first mention of the monastery on Skellig Michael, Co. Kerry, was when Vikings raided it in 824, but it was probably founded before 700 AD. As well St Michael, two early-Irish saints are referred to: St Fintán and St Suibhne, who may have been its founder.

The only traces of the Irish monks now to be found in Iceland are some manmade caves with crosses engraved into their walls and a few place names incorporating *papa*, an early-Irish word for a priest or monk. The account of the *Voyage of St Brendan*, a sixth-century explorer monk, describes him seeing a volcano erupting: 'a great hellish mountain which appeared full of clouds and smoke about its summit … of an appalling height and full of firebrands and red sparks'. This must be based upon accounts of actual Icelandic volcanic eruptions, but sadly the *Voyage* was written down after the Vikings had reached Iceland, so was not necessarily from an early-Irish monk's tale.[63]

Viking leaders set themselves up as Irish kings, with their towns as capitals, and introduced the first Irish coinage. The first notable king of Dublin was Ímhair (Norse Ivar), who was described as the 'king of all the Norse of Ireland and Britain' when he died in 873. His control over the Norse settlements of the Irish Sea and western Scotland did not last; the Irish-Norse leaders were constantly feuding and were expelled from Ireland in 902. They retreated to their bases in northern Britain but returned in 914 with a large fleet led by two of Ímhair's descendants, Ragnald and Sihtric Cáech, and recaptured Waterford.

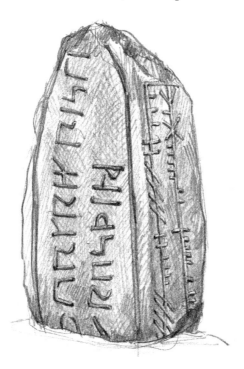

Part of a high cross from Killaloe, Co. Clare. The inscription in runes and ogham declares that Thorgrim, presumably its Norse abbot, had carved it.

Three years later in 917 Sihtric defeated the Uí Néill high king, Niall Glundubh, at Tara and retook Wexford, Limerick and Dublin. He was now king of all the Irish Viking territories, as well as the Isle of Man. Ragnall then took York, the Viking capital of northern England and, after he died in 921, Sihtric handed Dublin over to a kinsman and himself became king of York, creating a real Irish-Viking empire. Sihtric died in 927 and his son succeeded. After his death in 941 their empire fell apart, but Dublin remained a powerful Viking city.

The Vikings made many positive contributions to Ireland. They founded its first towns, introduced currency, developed trade and gave Irish useful new words, such as *fuinneog*, a window, and *long*, a ship. This melding of cultures even has a bilingual memorial. On a tenth- or eleventh-century cross fragment at Killaloe in County Clare, an Irish ogham inscription stands beside an Old Norse one in 'short-twig' runes: 'BEANDACHT [AR] TOROQR [IM], *A Blessing upon Thorgrim*' and '[Þ]URGRIM RISTI [K]RUS ÞINA, *Thorgrim carved this cross.*' This is Ireland's only runic inscription. The Vikings ruled this area after founding Limerick in the ninth century, abbots were often related to local rulers, and commissioned many high crosses. At Monasterboice, a monastery inside the Viking kingdom of Dublin, a tenth-century cross is inscribed, 'ÓR DO MUIRE-DACH LAS NDERNAD IN CHROS, *Pray for Muiredach who had this cross made.*'

RATHS AND SOUTERRAINS

The most typical features of settlements in the early-Christian period were circular ring forts or raths, and houses were round, as they had been since Neolithic times. Some had stone walls, but more commonly they were made from two layers of woven withies starting at ground level, and brought together at the top to make a domed roof. Bracken was packed between the layers, mud daub slapped on the outside, the roof was thatched, and there was a central hearth for cooking and warmth. These yurt-like structures could be thrown up quickly and renewed every few years, often by burning, as this got rid of lice, fleas and vermin.

Grander roundhouses had doors with stout wooden frames. These were probably elaborately decorated, as early law codes have heavy penalties for defacing them, and they were removed when houses were demolished. Raths had imposing entrances with heavy wooden gates, and their banks were fronted with dry-stone revetments topped by palisading. Inside, seats doubled as beds and consisted of timbers jammed against the sides with the space between filled with plant material. It was easy to lose small objects and during an excavation of the Deerpark Farm rath in County Antrim a glass bead with gold inlay was found in one bed. It is identical to beads on the Ardagh Chalice, so someone must have had a precious object here, such as a fine brooch from the same workshop.

The raths often had defensive features called souterrains, stone-lined underground rooms with connecting passages that made twists, turns and level changes. They were probably hideaways during attacks, particularly for anyone who might be seized by raiders. Valuables and pottery have also been found in them. Gangs of souterrain builders moved around the country, and a standard tariff was laid down. They were not an Irish invention, however: the Armoricans had made the earliest-known examples, before the idea spread to Britain and Ireland.

MORTAR AND MINARETS

Ardmore, Co. Waterford, was supposedly founded by Declán, a member of the local royal house, the Déisi Muman, who was active before St Patrick.

Earlier Irish churches were wooden and often replaced. The Irish could not build stone churches, apart from some tiny dry-stone oratories, until they learnt about mortar technology from the Anglo-Saxons in the eighth century. Considerable resources and expertise were required to create mortar, so the first Irish stone and mortar churches were built under royal patronage. These were plain buildings with tiny windows and few features, unlike those of England or the continent, but even so were a major step forward. Several royal patrons also employed the builders to raise stone and mortar houses for themselves near the monasteries at Clonmacnoise, Armagh and Cashel, which were secular as well as religious capitals.

Around 900, the major monasteries also started to build *clog tigh*, bell towers. The Irish examples were all round, mostly about a hundred feet high, and had a peculiar background. Charlemagne had instituted houses for the Irish pilgrims, and two were in Ravenna, the richest Italian town of the time, whose spectacular Byzantine churches now housed monastic communities.

Ravenna's enormous harbour, Classe, was once the headquarters of Roman and Byzantine fleets. The Ravennans also maintained a fleet and traded regularly with Alexandria in Islamic Egypt. At its harbour entrance was the Pharos lighthouse, which, at over 500 feet, was the tallest building in the world. Its top storey collapsed in an earthquake, so the Muslims rebuilt it as a tall round tower, and used it for calling out the hours of prayer. As the Muslims expanded their control westwards, they built scaled-down versions of the Pharos – round towers on a square base – on the corners of the *ribats*, the rectangular forts they built at other harbours. They called these towers *minarets* from the Arabic word for a lighthouse.

The Ravennans were impressed by this idea. They built a round tower beside the church at the entrance to Classe and used it, like the Pharos tower, both as a sightline for ships and as the place to broadcast the holy hours. The Ravennans, however, installed bells rather than muezzins, and by the end of the ninth century many of the monasteries in Ravenna had their own round bell towers. The Irish in Ravenna must then have got word home, for by the tenth century Irish monasteries were also building round bell towers beside their churches.[64]

Nearly all the Irish round towers have doors raised well above ground level. This made them reasonably secure, as access depended on removable wooden ladders. Unfortunately, their wooden interiors made them vulnerable to fire. The Lector of Slane, amongst others, was burnt when the 'Foreigners of Dublin' torched its tower in 949, and when Connor MacFergal Ó Lochlainn burnt the tower at Trim in 1127, 'many people suffered martyrdom'. In 1156, Muirchertach Mac Niall Mac Lochlainn set fire to Fertagh's round tower along with the monastry's 'chief master', and later still, Tighernan Ua Ruairc burnt the round tower at Tullyard in Meath, 'full of people'. Probably the most dramatic round-tower death was in 1076 when Murchadh, son of Conchobhar Uí Maelseachlainn, the newly elected Irish high king, was murdered by Amhlaidh, king of the Gailenga, in the Kells round tower. Many treasures also met their end in these burnings. St Patrick's crosier and other relics went up in flames in Slane's tower in 949, as did copies of the scriptures, relics, vestments and bells at Monasterboice in 1097.[65]

These round towers are called *clog tigh* in Irish, bell houses, and ringing bells for monastic hours remained their primary purpose, but their height and the effort required to build them meant they were also statements of wealth and power. A tower was built at Armoy in County Antrim, for example, because its monastery was at the royal citadel of the Irish kingdom of Dalriada; there is another at Kilkenny, the seat of the kings of Ossory (*Osraigh*). Round towers embellished many other royal monasteries, too.

HIGH KINGS AND THEIR RIVALS

Chariots and their riders carved on a cross at Clonmacnoise, Co. Offaly.

During the early-Christian period, the many Irish kings increasingly became independent powers although tribal significance and power persisted. A king had to be physically perfect and in some places still went through ritual marriage to a local sovereignty goddess. A royal hierarchy also gradually arose; the king of a *tuath* (the smallest unit) was subordinate to a greater local king who in turn was under a regional overlord. He generally had power over much of one of the old tribal 'Fifths' of Ireland, Ulster, Munster, Connacht, Leinster and Meath. Ultimately, in the seventh to ninth centuries, the concept of an *ard rí* developed, a high king with some level of authority over all other Irish kings. This was linked to the ancient tribal capital of Tara and to *Mídh*, Meath, whose central position had been important since the days of the great megalithic tombs.

The northern and southern Uí Neill, the descendants of Niall Noígiallach in Ulster and Mídh, were the first to use the *ard rí* (high king) title, but other powerful regional dynasties resisted their pretensions. The first of these were the Eóganacht of Munster. Once the Vikings were established in the south, Eóganacht power waned, but another Munster line, the Dál Cais of the lower Shannon basin, soon took their place. The first successful member of this family was Cennétig mac Lorcáin, who became king of north Munster in 951. His eldest son extended control over eastern Munster and the 'Ostmen', the Vikings, of Limerick and Waterford, and when he died in 976 his brother, Brian Boru, became king.

Brian Boru intended to emulate Charlemagne. He had a standing army, won the backing of the Church as well as the Wexford Vikings and extended his rule across Leinster and Munster. The Uí Neill high king, Máel Sechnaill, then allied himself with Brian, recognizing him in 997 as king of the southern half of the country, the *Leth Moga*, and two years later they jointly defeated the powerful Dublin Ostmen. Finally, in 1002, Máel Sechnaill conceded his position as high king to Brian.

Brian now called himself emperor of Ireland, but in the end his ambitions failed. In 1013, a minor Uí Neill king rebelled against Máel Sechnaill, who ruled Ulster as Brian's ally, and a year later the kings of Leinster joined with the Dublin Ostmen to defy Brian. He attacked his opponents at Clontarf, near Dublin, and broke them, but he was also killed in the battle.

Máel Sechnaill now became high king again but once he died the country fell into a tangle of power struggles. There was now a new breed of provincial kings. Just like European or Anglo-Saxon rulers they had retinues and standing armies, promulgated laws, imposed taxes, held personal estates and made formal land grants.

Forty years later, another national figure emerged. The Leinster king, Diarmat mac Máil na mBó, took Dublin in 1052 and made himself its king. He then drove the Uí Neill high king out and assumed the title, ruling much as Brian had done, and maintaining a formal court.

After Diarmat was killed ten years later, Brian Boru's grandson became high king and was succeeded by his son, Muirchertach. Neither could subdue the Ulster Uí Néills, but they ruled over most of the rest of the country. Muirchertach even made alliances with the Norwegians and Normans, and encouraged the introduction of the Gregorian movement that was disentangling the Church from the European power system, and abolished married clergy. The Ostmen of Dublin, Limerick and Waterford had already introduced these reforms, thanks to their contacts with the English Normans, and their bishops swore allegiance to the Archbishop of Canterbury. Muirchertach wanted Ireland to be a modern state with a national Church, and so called two synods, introduced Gregorian reforms and gave Armagh ecclesiastical primacy. By the time Muirchertach died in 1119, a powerful Uí Neill king, Domnall Mac Lochlainn, had again appeared in the north. He became high king but died soon afterwards so his brother, Muirchertach Mac Lochlainn, took his place.

There was, however, a rival power. Connacht had risen in importance and prosperity thanks to improved weather conditions, and its king, Toirrdelbach Ua Conchobhair (Turlough O'Connor), was highly ambitious. He imitated Norman methods of rule, kept a large standing army, had the Ostmen's fleets at his disposal, and built bridges and castles. These were of the Norman motte and bailey variety – earthen banks, ditches and mounds topped by wooden palisades. He conquered Munster and divided it in two, giving the western half to the Ua Briains, the O'Briens, and the eastern portion to the MacCarthaighs, the MacCarthys. However, the high king, Muirchertach Mac Lochlainn, was not to be suppressed.

EMULATING EUROPE

Cormac's Chapel, Cashel, Co. Tipperary,
the most outstanding pre-Norman example
of Romanesque architecture in Ireland.

Toirrdelbach's methods of control were radical. He ejected rival kings from their territories and divided their lands among his supporters, effectively introducing proper feudalism, where the monarch owned his kingdom and granted estates to his subjects. They could then be expelled at will. Other Irish kings also emulated modern European ways. When Toirrdelbach reinstated Cormac MacCarthaigh as king of Munster in 1127, Cormac had a grand European-style church built at Cashel, his citadel. His cousin was the abbot of Regensburg in Germany, which the Irish had founded only sixteen years earlier. Its 'Irish Church', the Schottenkirche, was finished and two of its builders came over. Cashel's church has similar towers but looks more like Murbach in Alsace. The ribbed vault was an English innovation.

Cormac's Chapel was the wonder of Ireland. Many churches were built over the following decades, but none had its quality, apart from a little church at Rahan in County Offaly and Temple Finghin at Clonmacnoise. The latter was also commissioned by a king. It had a vaulted interior and fine stonework, but the overall design is clumsy. Rahan, on the other hand, is a fine piece of architecture and some features have an oddly Near Eastern feel. We know that

Armenian monks had once lived nearby, refugees from Islam's spread, and perhaps elements of their culture were absorbed by a local school of masons.

A twelfth-century pillar from Rahan church, Co. Offaly.

Figure holding griffins on White Island, Lough Erne, Co. Fermanagh, one of seven carved c.800–1000 AD, and mostly wearing the long tunics of churchmen. They may have been intended either to support a pulpit or the beams of a wooden church.

Church architecture in Armenia, Georgia and the Middle East was remarkably sophisticated, and even Charlemagne employed an Armenian architect for his most adventurous churches. Rahan benefited from this same infusion, with its curiously oriental half-columns and their bulbous bases, which also appear in the Nun's Church at Clonmacnoise.

Most of the new ideas coming into Ireland, however, were western European ones. On Regensburg's Schottenkirche full-frontal heads stare down from Cashel's facade as they do at Ardmore and Clonfert, and the full-length caryatids of its arcading resemble the stone figures of White Island on Lough Erne. The Vikings introduced Scandinavian decorative styles, and many Irish stone carvings and metalwork are a riot of interlace and interwoven, elongated animals.

*St Patrick's Bell Shrine. It was commis-
sioned by Domhnaill MacAmhlaigh,
Archbishop of Armagh in the 1090s.*

The European monastic orders were in great demand. In 1126, the first Augustinian house in Ireland was founded in Erenagh in County Down, followed the
next year by Cormac's Chapel and a Savignac monastery in the Irish midlands.
Then, *c*.1130, an Augustinian priory arose near St Patrick's Purgatory on Station
Island at Lough Derg, followed by another in Fermanagh, and over the next two
decades English Savignac monks, French Cistercians and Augustinian nuns set
up houses in Dublin. The Cistercians opened a house in Kerry in 1151, and then
Mellifont Abbey, County Louth, in 1157.

Mellifont was the first Irish monastery built to the standard European
formula with church, cloisters and domestic buildings forming an integrated
architectural ensemble. Malachy, the bishop of Armagh, was the driving force.
In 1140, he visited the new Cistercian abbey of Clairvaux on his way to Rome to
be confirmed as archbishop and Irish primate and was so impressed that he left
some of his entourage there. Two years later, a team from Clairvaux arrived
and founded Mellifont. At its dedication in 1157 Malachy officiated, attended by
two more archbishops, the high king, Muirchertach Mac Lochlainn, and several
lesser kings. Within the year, the Benedictines had founded Jerpoint in Kilkenny
and the Augustinians Ferns priory in County Wexford. A dozen Cistercian
abbeys followed, and, being talented agriculturalists, they created rural markets
and boosted the countryside's prosperity.

While this ecclesiastical modernization was underway, a tough political power struggle was going on. When Toirrdelbach died in 1156, his son Ruaidrí took over, but Muirchertach Mac Lochlainn invaded Connacht in 1159 and continuted to inflict damage until Ruaidrí recognized him as high king.

When Mac Lochlainn was killed in 1166, Ruaidrí marched to Dublin and gave the Ostmen four thousand cows to let him be inaugurated as high king in their cathedral. All previous inaugurations were at tribal assembly sites, so a European-style coronation performed in the cathedral of the country's major city by an archbishop gave him the same sacred Christian authority as Norman or other European feudal rulers. Even so, Ruaidrí left Dublin as soon as it was over to hold a traditional inauguration at Teltown in Meath.

Killeshin doorway, Co. Laois. This was one of the
churches erected by Diarmat Mac Murchadha.

In spite of this concession to old ways, Ruaidrí demonstrated his modernity at Teltown by giving land grants and promulgating laws. There was, however, a dark cloud on the horizon. Ruaidrí had expelled the Leinster king, Diarmat Mac Murchadha, from his territory, but Diarmat was not easily beaten. He, too, was a man of the modern world, who had not only been born in Dublin (its Norse king was his uncle) but also maintained a mansion there.[66] He had built an impressive new church at Killeshin, and brought Augustinian monks over from Bristol to set up a house at his capital, Ferns. Their church followed the latest Romanesque model, with two towers flanking its west facade.[67] In return for supporting Henry II of England in his campaign on the British west coast, Diarmat now sought his help.

v. *The Normans and After*

The Normans and After

— 1170. Strongbow and 30 Norman knights land and reinstate Diarmat Mac Murchadha. The Normans take Dublin.

1171. Diarmat dies. Strongbow becomes ruler of Leinster and the Normans expand their conquest. Henry II lands and tries to bring the Norman knights under control.

— 1170–1250. Normans conquer two-thirds of Ireland.

— 1315–18. Bruce invasions. Finally defeated at Dundalk.

— 1348–9. Black Death strikes Ireland.

— 1366. Statutes of Kilkenny try to prevent the colonists 'degenerating' into Irish ways.

— 1394–9. Richard II visits Ireland twice and tries to bring the country under his control.

— Post-1399, Ireland becomes a land of two nations – the English Pale and the Irish lordships go their separate ways. Period of aristocratic control. The Earls of Kildare become the dominant rulers of the Pale as lord's deputies from 1470.

1537. Eighth Earl of Kildare, his son and brothers executed for opposing Henry VIII's break with the pope.

— 1589. Spanish Armada.

— Hugh O'Neill, Earl of Tyrone, goes into rebellion.

— 1602. Battle of Kinsale.

DIARMAT

Having visited Henry in France, where he was campaigning, and with permission to recruit from his fighting men, Diarmat Mac Murchadha went to south Wales. He knew many Norman knights there, having campaigned with them several years before. Richard fitz Gilbert, better known as Strongbow, agreed to organize a fighting force for Diarmat in return for marrying Diarmat's daughter, Aoife, and inheriting Leinster on his death. Two other knights set up the initial expedition, in exchange for Wexford, and Diarmat landed back in Ireland in August 1167 with one Norman knight, a Welsh prince and a few archers and sergeants.

In spite of bringing such a small troop, Diarmat rallied his supporters and was soon re-established as Leinster king. He came to terms with Ruaidrí Ua Conchobhair by handing over seven hostages, including a son, and a hundred ounces of gold for Ruaidrí's ally Ua Ruairc in recompense for abducting his wife years earlier. Diarmat settled back in Ferns and his Normans returned to Wales.

During the following year, however, Ruaidrí took back Meath, Munster and Dublin, and triumphantly held the Lughnasa fair at Teltown. Around this hill, in a landscape dotted with ancient earthworks, tumuli, rivers, lakes and ponds, Ireland's greatest annual fair took place. The high king presided, along with other rulers. Horsemen raced over hills and through woods, ponds and rivers; wrestling feats determined who was the strongest; herds of cattle were driven through the river and aquatic fights were staged. The high king gave out laws, judgments were made and contracts solemnized.

Ruaidrí tightened his grip during the autumn and winter of 1168–9. Diarmat therefore appealed once more to Strongbow and his friends. Henry had marginalized them for supporting Stephen fitz Harding in the succession dispute two decades earlier, so the prospect of acquiring unencumbered Irish territories was extremely tempting. In May, a Norman group landed near Wexford with forty knights and five hundred men; Diarmat brought five hundred more, and Wexford soon surrendered. Diarmat then dispatched part of his force to help his son-in-law, Domnall Mór Ua Briain, king of Thomond, drive Ruaidrí out of Munster.

To a large degree, the Normans' adaptability was the key to their success but they also had superior weaponry and the stirrup, the greatest technological breakthrough since horse riding had begun. The Irish did not have this technology, which required solidly framed saddles, so their cavalry was no match for the Normans, who wore chain mail and wielded tempered steel swords or lances.[68]

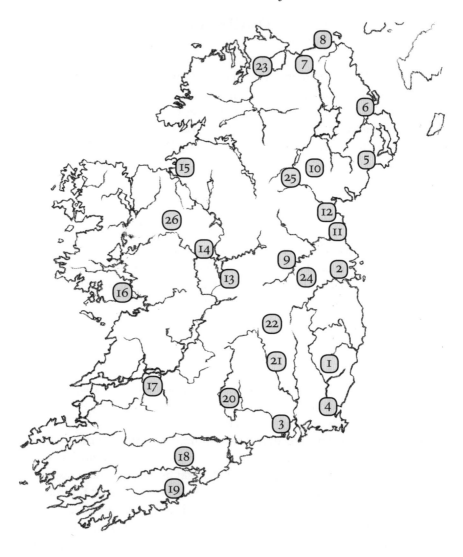

Strongbow himself arrived in August. Waterford soon fell and then Dublin, where the Normans lost patience and stormed the city while Diarmat was negotiating with its leaders. As the Dubliners had surrendered to Strongbow, he claimed the city for himself. Diarmat was not concerned, for with Strongbow's troops he drove Ruaidrí's allies out of Leinster and Meath, and then retired to winter in Ferns in County Wicklow.

Ferns was an impressive modern town. Diarmat had a stone and mortar castle and house there as well as several churches, and the new priory church rivalled Cormac's Chapel. It followed the latest European Romanesque style with two round bell towers rising from square bases framing its west facade like St Pantaleon's at Cologne. Diarmat ruled like a European feudal monarch with a large entourage and court, and his intention was to replace Ruaidrí as high king. In May 1171, however, he died and was buried at Ferns below a high cross.

Remains of the Augustinian abbey at Ferns, Co. Wexford, and the stump of the high cross erected over Diarmat Mac Murchadha's grave.

Dundrum initially consisted of an earth motte topped by a timber fort and a stone curtain wall constructed round the upper ward. It was built by John de Courcy soon after he invaded Ulster in 1177. After 1210, Hugh de Lacy added the round stone keep. It was one of the major Norman strongholds in the north of Ireland.

Clough motte, Co. Down, was a typical Anglo-Norman earthwork castle. On top of the motte a stone tower was later built, and there was also a large hall standing here in the fifteenth century.

After Diarmat's death, Strongbow became king of Leinster, but the Norse king of Dublin soon appeared with his fleet and almost retook the city before being captured and executed. Soon afterwards, Ruaidrí also besieged Dublin with a large army but, although he was outwitted, Diarmat Mac Murchadha's brother started gathering up a large army to retake Leinster, and Waterford's inhabitants threw out its Norman garrison. Other Irish kings were also negotiating for their own Norman warriors.

Henry II did not need any of his knights becoming independent Irish kings. He also urgently needed to appease the papal legates who were investigating Thomas à Becket's murder, so it was strategic to say that he would go to Ireland to institute Church reform. Henry met Strongbow in Wales in October 1171, and they landed near Waterford with an army of 4000 soldiers and 500 knights.

Strongbow then surrendered his Irish lands to Henry, who formally granted them to him as a feudal estate. The charters were drawn up, the wax seals attached, and Norman feudalism had arrived.

Many Irish kings did homage to Henry in the hope of achieving stability and Ruaidrí offered his fealty, as was acceptable between equals. Henry had a wattle and wood palace constructed by Irish workmen outside Dublin, and entertained liberally throughout the following winter. (The Normans were amazed that the Irish could weave a palace out of withies, but the craftsmen adroitly adapted their roundhouse skills, just as they had for the Vikings.) A Church council was arranged, the hierarchy assembled, Gregorian reforms instigated and Henry was acknowledged as overlord of the Church in Ireland. This title had originally been offered to him by the pope fifteen years earlier.

Henry II left Ireland at Easter 1172, feeling he had imposed a degree of order. Strongbow's power was counterbalanced by de Lacy and de Courcy, who got equally large territories, and also by Ruaidrí, the acknowledged high king. In 1175, Ruaidrí sent his archbishop with other Church leaders to Henry in England, who confirmed Ruaidrí's position and agreed he should head the Irish kings in return for recognizing Henry as his liege lord.

Trim Castle, Co. Meath, was the largest Anglo-Norman castle in Ireland. It was constructed over a thirty-year period by Hugh de Lacy and his son Walter. Hugh was granted the Liberty of Meath by King Henry II in 1172 as part of his scheme to curb Strongbow's expansionist policies. The massive keep of c.1176 replaced an earlier wooden fortress.

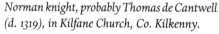

Norman knight, probably Thomas de Cantwell (d. 1319), in Kilfane Church, Co. Kilkenny.

Effigy of Margaret FitzGerald, daughter of the Earl of Kildare and wife of Piers Butler, eighth Earl of Ormonde in Gowran Abbey, Co. Kilkenny.

However, the Norman knights conquered on, building forts from Mount Sandel on the river Bann in the north to Tralee in the southwest. Henry had to issue new charters to cover these conquests and bring them under his control. More towns sprang up, including Galway, Drogheda, Kilkenny, Roscommon, Dundalk, Athlone, Trim and Sligo, and the land was split into manorial holdings. Each was to have a manor house and a church, and the villagers got strips in three large fields, a pattern that already worked well in England and France.

A network of market towns also grew up, each within a day's journey of the surrounding villages, creating Ireland's familiar rural landscape. Woods were felled, agricultural production soared, grain and timber were exported, wool-bearing sheep were introduced[69] and trade boomed. However, Ireland's population was small, so land-hungry people from England came to boost the numbers. Most were from the West Country, and introduced now familiar Irish family names, including Bermingham, Bourke, Stafford, Luttrell, Wogan, Cody, Joyce, Preston, Sarsfield, Dillon and Wilde.

There was considerable resistance to the Normans, but they did bring stability and order. Ruaidrí was deposed and reinstated several times and many other Irish rulers enthusiastically adopted the Norman approach including Domnall Mór Ó Briain, king of Munster, who founded nine European-style monasteries and three Romanesque cathedrals.

The only serious attempt to drive the Normans out was made by Brian O'Neill of Ulster in the mid-thirteenth century. He declared himself high king and attacked the Normans in 1259 but died in their first battle. After this, opposition was limited to piecemeal actions by individual Irish lords.

There was, however, a positive consequence of Brian O'Neill's disastrous campaign. One supporter, Aed O'Connor, heir to the Connacht king, married the daughter of MacSumharlaidhe, Lord of the Isles. She brought with her a hundred and sixty 'gallowglass'[70] fighting men, who followed the Viking custom of wearing chain mail and helmets, and of fighting with battle-axes or two-handed steel swords. Being as well armed as the Normans, gallowglass companies were very effective and were soon in demand all over Ireland. Several west-Scottish families transported them to Ireland in their boats, most notably the MacSuibhnes (MacSweenys) of Kintyre, the MacCabas (McCabes) from Argyll and the MacDonalds of the Isles. Their young men often became 'gallowglass captains' for Irish rulers, supplying them with fighting men as required.

Miniature effigy of a Norman knight on horseback, found in Hexham in Northumbria.

LOUGH DERG

An early map of Ireland showing St Patrick's Purgatory, Lough Derg, Co. Donegal, as a large feature, indicating its unusual significance in the Middle Ages.

Although the Irish Normans maintained a European lifestyle in their castles, manors, monasteries and walled towns, Irish ways continued elsewhere. Traditional customs were observed at holy wells, seasonal festivals took place on the hills, people gathered at old assembly places and pilgrimages were made to ancient shrines. The old Irish myths and epics were still recited.

On an island in Lough Derg, Co. Donegal, a great medieval pilgrimage centre developed. St Patrick had supposedly come here to perform acts of penance and to be shut into a stone-lined underground passageway leading to an inner chamber so as to see the horrors of Hell. As a result it was called St Patrick's Purgatory and the devout came here from all over Europe. It became so famous that early maps make it look extraordinarily large. After fasting and praying for fourteen days, the pilgrims were shut into the Purgatory for a day and a night, and the account of one twelfth-century visitor, Knight Owen, was a medieval bestseller. Dante even used its descriptions in his *Inferno* a hundred years later.

When Knight Owen was put into the Purgatory he met four white-robed figures who admonished him for his sins. Demons led him down to Hell, where some devils were driving red-hot nails into damned souls while others were boiled or frozen into icicles, squashed by vast toads, or bound to burning wheels. He then went to a crag where icy winds blew others into pools of foul water and demons stamped on them while howls and screams came from the Pit of the Damned. Knight Owen finally slithered over the Bridge of Impossibilities to see a locked door to Heaven, and get a distant glimpse of Paradise.

The Purgatory was completely destroyed in the 1630s but the descriptions of it indicate that this was a megalithic passage grave. Moreover, the practice of putting initiates through long periods of fasting, ritual observances and sleep deprivation followed by enclosure in a dark, underground place was typical of the hallucination-inducing processes used in shamanistic cultures. Knight Owen's account brings us as close as we can ever get to the Neolithic rites performed and the visions seen at Ireland's great megalithic sites.

The 'Ornecnus' inscribed stone from Station Island, Lough Derg, Co. Donegal, the site of the original St Patrick's Purgatory. It appears to be a Roman inscription, suggesting that this was a venerated place long before Christianity's arrival.

THE BRUCE INTERVENTION

St Laurence's Gate, Drogheda, Co. Louth, is the finest surviving fortified town gate in Ireland. It was originally three storeys high, but two more were added in the fifteenth century.

An uneasy stalemate continued between the Irish and Norman spheres of control until the early 1300s, when the balance was upset by Robert the Bruce. He had frustrated Edward I's attempts to control Scotland, and destroyed Edward II's army at Bannockburn in 1314 before turning to Ireland. He knew Ulster well, and was related to several leading Ulster families including the O'Neill kings of Tyrone and the de Burgo earls of Ulster. He was also related to the MacDonald Lords of the Isles who were an essential link in his plans as their fleets of galleys – direct descendants of the Vikings' boats – allowed him to move large numbers of men and supplies from Scotland to Ireland. The O'Neills offered the kingship of Ireland to Robert's brother Edward, the MacDonalds provided both men and boats, and the Bruce invasion landed in 1315.

Edward Bruce campaigned vigorously. He was crowned high king in 1316, Robert brought in more men to support him, many Norman manors, towns and villages were destroyed and in 1317 Dublin nearly fell. Yet although they penetrated as far as Limerick they could not break their opponents. By ill luck the climate deteriorated badly in 1315, and there were several years of harvest failure and bad winters. The Bruces' Irish campaigns unfortunately coincided with the appalling weather that caused the Great Famine of 1315–17. Millions died throughout northern Europe. It was the beginning of five centuries of global climatic downturn now called the Little Ice Age. As a result, the Bruces' armies only survived by expropriating food and livestock from the native population.

In 1318 the Bruces' forces were beaten at Dundalk, and Edward Bruce was killed. This ended Ireland's last chance of being an independent feudal state, but despite their victory, Anglo-Norman power declined. The invaders had wrecked their lands, many settlers returned to England and several Irish families now wrested their lands back, including the O'Neills, who gained much of eastern Ulster.

Thirty years later, the Black Death struck. It was particularly virulent where English and Norman settlers lived in densely packed villages and towns, and the monastic annals of Kilkenny described it as the end of humanity. The settlers abandoned many smaller places, and the surviving great Norman families took to living by Irish laws and customs, which gave them much greater power. The de Burgos of Connacht, for example, denied having any feudal obligations at all to the English Crown.

Dungiven, Co. Derry, the fourteenth-century Gothic tomb of an O'Cahan chieftain. Below him in six niches are armed warriors wearing kilts. These are 'gallowglasses', or Scottish mercenary warriors.

In Wicklow, a McMurrough descendant of the Mac Murchadhas was installed as king of Leinster in 1327 and vowed to take back Dublin. Such inaugurations became the norm as old Irish families reasserted their power. English law no longer operated beyond the Pale, the English-speaking areas around Dublin, Drogheda and Dundalk, but, in fact, as the fourteenth century progressed, increasing numbers within the Pale were also native Irish. The 1366 Statutes of Kilkenny, which prohibited settlers from marrying into native families, using the Irish tongue or wearing Irish dress, were little more than an expression of despair.

Governing Ireland was now only a burden. Richard II came over twice in the 1390s to receive homage just as Henry II had done, but he was deposed soon after his second visit, and as England dissolved into the Wars of the Roses, Ireland was largely left to its own devices. Even so, some prosperity returned; castles were built as much for comfort as defence, and many Third Order Franciscan houses sprang up. These friars used the language of the people, Irish, not Latin, to spread God's Word, so their popularity shows the strength of the Irish revival. The country's administration was in the hands of great Norman-Irish magnates, particularly the FitzGeralds and Butlers. These were 'over-mighty lords' with vast possessions and similar outlooks to their English counterparts, who fought furiously throughout the fifteenth century, until Henry Tudor's (Henry VII) victory at Bosworth in 1485 ended their world.

Adare Friary, Co. Limerick, a fine example of the type of friary erected by the Third Order Franciscans in the fourteenth and fifteenth centuries.

ARISTOCRATIC CONTROL

The eighth and ninth Earls of Kildare, chiefs of the FitzGerald family, were the appointed royal administrators of Ireland in the late fifteenth century. They used Irish methods of rule and so their tenantry was obliged, amongst other things, to provide food and lodging for their private standing armies. They thus controlled Leinster, enriched themselves and protected the Pale at a minimal cost to the English Crown. They had a network of alliances with other Irish lordships, were closely related to many, and ruled like petty kings. Inside the Pale some English norms continued, but when the English Crown tried to impose its will, the balance fell apart.

The first crisis happened soon after Henry VII came to power. Some English Lancastrians put up Lambert Simnel as the rightful King Edward VI, brought him to Ireland with an army of two thousand men and won the eighth Earl of Kildare's backing. He summoned a parliament that recognized Simnel as King Edward, and he was crowned in Dublin's Christ Church Cathedral. Four and a half thousand Irish mercenaries, mostly *kerns*, lightly clad but highly mobile infantry, were assembled. Simnel's army and additional troops embarked for England in 1487 and successfully beat all the local militia groups, but were decisively defeated by Henry VII's army at Stoke Field, near Newark in Nottinghamshire.

In spite of his involvement, Kildare survived. Ireland's potential as a launch pad for attacking Henry had been demonstrated, and the second pretender, Perkin Warbeck, came to Ireland from Spain in 1494. Warbeck found support amongst Kildare's rivals in Munster, and although Kildare suppressed this rebellion, Henry replaced Kildare with a high-ranking Englishman, Sir Edward Poynings, and provided him with several thousand soldiers.

Poynings replaced all the local officials, the 'Old English' gentry of the Pale, with his English entourage and called a parliament to enact 'Poynings' Law'. This stated that the Irish parliament's Acts would only become law if passed by the English parliament as well, and that all English Acts applied to Ireland. When the money ran out, however, Poynings and his army were called back and Kildare returned to power.

When Henry VIII broke with Rome, he needed Ireland's agreement. The ninth Earl of Kildare, however, violently opposed Henry's divorce, and in 1534 was summoned to London. Kildare left his son, Lord Offaly, in charge. When he heard that his father was in the Tower, he marched with his private army into Dublin and denounced Henry VIII publicly. As he was now in open rebellion, the

Holy Roman Emperor, Charles V, offered him help. It was the first time that a European power had tried to undermine the English by supporting Irish rebels.

Henry appointed Sir William Skeffington his new lord deputy. He had already served as Henry's deputy in Ireland for three years, and had an army of several thousand men, so he knew what to do and went to work remorselessly. Offaly's support collapsed, and he was taken to London with five uncles, where all were executed in February 1537. The ninth Earl of Kildare had already died of his infirmities in the Tower in 1534.

Maynooth Castle, Co. Kildare, was originally built by the FitzGeralds in the twelfth century. In 1426, the sixth Earl of Kildare rebuilt it as the family's main seat and stronghold. An English force led by William Skeffington bombarded it in March 1535 during Lord Offaly's rebellion and reduced much of it to rubble. After ten days its garrison surrendered and was subsequently executed.

ENGLISH RULE

Dunluce, Co. Antrim. It was the strongest north-Ulster stronghold in native hands in the fifteenth and sixteenth centuries. The MacDonalds of Islay held it from the mid-sixteenth century to facilitate their importation of fighting men from the Scottish Highlands and Islands for the Irish wars.

Having abandoned the old system of rule in Ireland, the English had to find other methods. Initially, they tried negotiating with each lordship, demanding that Irish lords adopt English dress, laws, customs and language in return for having the rights of English landowners, but Henry was in a hurry. He replaced his papal title of 'Lord of the Irish' with 'King of Ireland' and treated Ireland as part of his English domain.

The native magnates opposed this, but there was no going back. Colonies were founded and abandoned, the eleventh Earl of Kildare (grandson of the ninth Earl who died in the Tower in 1534) returned in the late 1550s to keep the Pale quiet, and the Irish of Gaelic and Norman ancestry held onto Catholicism to demonstrate their opposition.

Elizabeth Tudor (Elizabeth I) also had plans for colonies and conquest, but had too few resources. The English garrisons mounted expeditions, destroyed forts and wasted swathes of countryside, but they could not hold the country down. The old families simply bounced back, and Ireland remained a patch-work of interconnected lordships. The major problem was Ulster, where Shane O'Neill maintained his family's power. He was happy enough to visit Eliza-beth's court in London in 1562, but continued ruling in the old Irish way. In the end he was defeated by the O'Donnells, and then murdered by his Scottish gallowglass suppliers, the MacDonalds, in revenge for the death in his custody of their own chieftain, the last claimant to be a Lord of the Isles. They left O'Neill's body in a shallow grave so that English troops could send his head to Dublin. A new O'Neill arose, but the MacDonalds now had control of the north-Antrim coastline, allowing them to import more fighting men from the Highlands and Islands.

Ormond Castle, Carrick-on-Suir, Co. Tipperary, the only Irish Elizabethan mansion to survive, was a seat of the Earls of Ormonde.

In the 1570s, the pope excommunicated Elizabeth and declared it the duty of all Catholics to depose her. A small expedition backed by the pope landed at Smerwick, Co. Kerry, in 1578. It found support in Leinster and Munster, led by the Earl of Desmond, and there were upheavals in Ulster and Connacht. This was the greatest crisis since Kildare's rebellion, and a new lord deputy, Lord Grey, arrived with 6500 men. Grey relied on brutality. He executed those who surrendered, destroyed harvests, slaughtered cattle and by the time of his recall in 1582 there was even famine in the Pale. Munster's condition was the worst: 'In short space there were almost none left and a most populous and plentiful country suddenly void of man or beast,' wrote Edmund Spenser in his *A View* (1633).

Carraigahowley Castle, Co. Mayo. Seat of Granuaile, pirate queen of Mayo and Connacht.

Red Bay Motte and Bailey, Co. Antrim, a Norman motte with a sixteenth-century tower house built on it by the MacDonalds. The beach below was a perfect landing place for their galleys.

Desmond was sent to the Tower and English settlers descended on his territory. When Armada ships foundered on Ireland's coasts a few years later, the great potential of Spanish power inspired some Irish leaders to beg Philip II of Spain to take Ireland under his wing. Hugh O'Neill, Earl of Tyrone, briefly considered if Philip might appoint him Irish king under the Spanish Crown, but instead they asked Philip to appoint his nephew, Archduke Albert, the governor of the Netherlands, as his representative. Emboldened by the prospect of Spanish aid, O'Neill and his confederates openly rebelled in 1595. The O'Donnells captured Sligo and north Connacht, and the O'Neills not only dominated Ulster but even routed a regular English army at the Battle of the Yellow Ford in 1598.

It began to look as if Tudor power might evaporate. Hugh Roe O'Donnell and Hugh O'Neill held Ulster and Connacht, the Munster plantation was destroyed, the Leix–Offaly colony despoiled, and they headed a coalition of Irish and Old English magnates. O'Donnell's and O'Neill's forces could now move freely through the country, and the properties of any remaining supporters of Elizabeth were enthusiastically destroyed.

However, this success largely resulted from Elizabeth's decision to appoint her court favourite, Lord Essex, a useless fighting man, as her Irish deputy. When a more seasoned soldier, Mountjoy, replaced him in early 1600 with 13,200 men at his disposal, he soon confined Tyrone to his Ulster heartland, and destroyed his forts, stores and cattle.

Desmond Castle, Kinsale, Co. Cork. It is the only building in the town that retains much of its original appearance from the time of the Spaniards' occupation in 1602.

Cahir Castle, Cahir, Co. Tipperary, the fortress of the Lords Cahir, a branch of the Butler family. Unlike the Ormondes they stayed Catholic and supported Hugh O'Neill, Earl of Tyrone, in his rebellion. Cahir was captured by the English in 1599 but later returned to Lord Cahir. It was surrendered in 1650 to Cromwell and two years later the Irish Confederate Wars officially ended when the articles of peace were signed here, and the last Lord Cahir died here in 1961.

In September 1601, Philip III of Spain sent 3400 troops to help the Irish. They landed at Kinsale in County Cork and Mountjoy moved south. By late October he was besieging Kinsale with 7000 men as Tyrone gathered his own forces. He arrived a few days before Christmas with 6400 men, and his victory looked certain as the English were weak with scurvy and dysentery.

The English, however, had one great advantage – heavy horses. The Spaniards had also arrived with equipment for a cavalry regiment, but the Irish only had ponies or small horses, not the weight-bearing animals required for armoured men with seventeen-and-a-half foot lances. Tyrone's cavalrymen could only wear leather jerkins and carry short pikes, which were as useless against heavy cavalry as toothpicks. Seeing the Irish advance, the English cavalrymen charged with their foot soldiers close behind, and within half an hour they had destroyed the Irish army. This consisted of virtually all their available fighting men, meaning that the defeat was fatal.

Mountjoy was soon back in the north destroying cattle, stores and castles. Famine followed and Ulster's leaders sued for peace. They were, as usual, given their old territories back as private estates held under the Crown, but only five years later, in 1607, most of them fled abroad on a small ship led by Hugh O'Neill, the Earl of Tyrone, and Hugh Roe O'Donnell, the Earl of Tyrconnell. This so-called Flight of the Earls emptied Ulster of its old ruling class. They could not cope with being James I's subjects or submitting to his laws, taxes and officials. Their vast properties were confiscated and the few who stayed mostly lost their lands through mismanagement or rebellion. English-speaking Britons acquired these Irish estates and crowds of land-hungry Lowland Scots poured into Ulster. They brought not only their language and Calvinist faith but also the horse collar and the ploughshare. These allowed them to plough the rich valley soils, leaving the lighter hill soils to the natives and their spades. It was a new otherness.

A horse collar. This was one of the most important pieces of equipment brought into Ulster in the Plantation period.

Man with horse ploughing on Rathlin Island, Co. Antrim, in the 1950s.

NOTES

1   Pierre Deschamps et al., 'Ice-sheet collapse and sea-level rise at the Bølling warming 14,600 years ago', *Nature*, 83, 7391, 29 March 2012. The possibility of an extraterrestrial impact being a cause of the Younger Drias cold period has long been debated, and has recently been confirmed. See Isabel Israde-Alcántara et al., 'Evidence from central Mexico supporting the Younger Dryas extraterrestrial impact hypothesis', Proceedings of the National Academy of Sciences, 5 March 2012. Apart from the consequent conflagrations in North America, there are indications that there were large forest fires in northwestern Europe as well.

2   The Irish Elk (*Megaloceros giganteus*) was a species of *Megaloceros* that ranged from Ireland to Siberia in the Late Pleistocene. It stood about 2.1m tall at the shoulders and had the largest antlers of any known cervid, with a maximum span of 3.65m and weighing up to 40kg. It matched the Alaskan moose (*Alces alces gigas*) in body size as the largest known deer. It is not clear exactly when they died out in Ireland but it was most probably during the Younger Dryas as there are no butchered elk remains at any Irish Mesolithic sites. This suggests that they had disappeared before any humans arrived.

3   See Amber Teacher, 'Irish Frogs may have Survived the Ice Age', *ZSL Institute of Zoology*, 17 March 2009.

4   Palaeolithic human societies used boats or rafts to cross quite wide bodies of water, as is evinced by stone tools found on Crete and other Mediterranean islands dating back to about 175,000 BC.

5   The last of these ice-melt floodings, the collapse of an enormous body of water dubbed Lake Agassiz in central Canada in 6200 BC, raised the sea level by 35cm. This extra weight of water probably caused the collapse of the continental shelf between Norway and Iceland and the subsequent tsunami that submerged the land bridge between Britain and Europe.

6   This subject has been dealt with extensively by David Lewis-Williams, *The Mind in the Cave* (London: Thames & Hudson 2002) and in David Lewis-Williams, *Inside the Neolithic Mind* (London: Thames & Hudson 2005).

7   Many human infectious diseases came from domesticated animals, from flu to smallpox.

8   Small sails were used in the Neolithic period, but propulsion was mostly done with paddles and oars. Grapes were first cultivated about 8000 BC in the Near East.

9   Patricia Balaresque et al., 'A Predominantly Neolithic Origin for European Paternal Lineages', *PLOS Biology*, 8 (1), 2010. Ötzi, the frozen pre-Bronze Age-period man found in the Italian Alps, belonged to the Mediterranean Neolithic line and was lactose intolerant.

10 Vicki Cumming, *A View from the West, the Neolithic of the Irish Sea Zone* (Oxford: Oxbow Books 2009).

11 All these plants were first cultivated in the Near East. Crab apples were collected by Mesolithic hunter-gatherers, including at Mount Sandel, but were presumably improved by Neolithic cultivation.

12 The causewayed enclosures have been recently dated with considerable accuracy. The first ones were created across the British Isles, northwestern France and Flanders *c.*3700, but were mostly abandoned within fifty years, Fifty years later more were built. A few were used for over a hundred years, some appear to have been attacked and destroyed, as many arrowheads were found near the burnt palisades. It is thought that these periods of enclosure building and their subsequent fate resulted from the faltering development of an organized tribal system.

13 The best overview of the prehistoric scene in Europe is Barry Cunliffe, *Europe Between the Oceans, Themes and Variations: 9000 BC–AD 1000* (New Haven and London: Yale University Press 2008).

14 See Chris Scarre, *Landscapes of Neolithic Brittany* (Oxford: OUP 2012).

15 Ballyalton was excavated by Estyn Evans and O. Davies in 1933.

16 The phrase 'Neolithic Dark Age' appears first in Aubrey Burl, *The Stone Circles of the British Isles* (New Haven and London: Yale University Press 1976). Michael Baillie of Queen's University Belfast, a leading dendrochronologist, has created a timeline for Ireland based upon bog-oak tree rings, which is accurate back to 5000 BC. It exposes the major periods of non-growth that indicate severe climatic disruptions. The earliest happened in 3195 BC and lasted ten years. See M. Baillie, *A Slice Through Time: Dendrochronology and Precision Dating* (London: Routledge 1995); M. Baillie, *Exodus to Arthur: Catastrophic Encounters with Comets* (London: NPI Media Group 1999); M. Baillie and Patrick McCafferty, *The Celtic Gods: Comets in Irish Mythology* (Stroud: Tempus 2001).

17 The temple complex is on a spit of land dividing two loughs: one fresh-water, the other sea. At each end of the spit is a large stone circle. The earliest calibrated radiocarbon date for the temple complex is 3200–3100 BC for part of the enormous walls surrounding the complex. This means it was erected soon after the 3195 BC volcanic eruption. Inside was a series of large stone buildings set up for ritual use. This complex is unprecedented and emphasizes Orkney's importance in Neolithic Europe. The temple was maintained for nine hundred years. The great passage tomb of Maes Howe was built close by three or four hundred years later. The buildings were demolished shortly after the next major volcanic eruption on Iceland in 2345 BC, and were replaced by a huge building that was used for just one enormous ritual feast involving the slaughtering of hundreds of cattle. The connection between this complex and volcanic event that seemed to threaten the death of the sun is therefore clear and must also apply to the other great structures put up soon after 3195 BC in Ireland and Britain. One of the circles and the Maes Howe tomb are oriented towards the midwinter solstice.

18 See Lewis-Williams, *Inside the Neolithic Mind*, and R. Rudgley, *The Alchemy of Culture* (London: British Museum Press 1993).

19 Other tombs at Locmariaquer use parts of other standing stones, presumably from the same alignment. There is uncertainty about what these curved shapes represent, but the Iberian sculpted forms resemble boomerangs. More are found being held by figurines in central Europe. See M. Gimbutas, *The Languages of the Goddess*

(San Francisco: HarperCollins Publishers 1991), pp. 4, 115, 194, 242, 288–9 & 308. The images carved on the standing stones have recently been reassessed, and these shapes identified as sperm whales.

20 The orientation of megalithic monuments was extremely varied. Some clearly looked at important features in the local landscape rather than having astronomical purposes and Cueva da Menga was created about 3700 BC. The cave in the mountain it pointed at was clearly of enormous importance as it was so elaborately painted.

21 Many Irish passage graves have recently been denuded of their quartz coverings.

22 See B. Smith and A. Walker, *Rock Art and Ritual, Mindscapes of Prehistory* (Stroud: Amberley Publishing 2011) and D. Lewis-Williams and D. Pearce, *Inside the Neolithic Mind* (London: Thames & Hudson, 2005).

23 The buried bowl was found in the early eighteenth century and has disappeared. It was described and illustrated in Molyneaux, *A Discourse Concerning the Danish Mounts, Forts and Towers in Ireland* (1725). See G. Stout, *Newgrange and the Bend of the Boyne* (Cork: CUP 2002), p. 48.

24 Only one quartzite block was found but the grooves scoring the upper surface of the lower lintel stone indicate that two blocks closed this opening and were moved in and out many times.

25 The stone at the entrance must have been designed to show those outside what lay within. The inner triple spiral was placed above the central bowl for the ashes of the dead and was lit by the sun at its maximum penetration: an act of fertilization or rebirth.

26 See T.F. O'Rahilly, *Early Irish History and Mythology* (Dublin 1946), pp. 117–29.

27 The terms 'tribes', 'septs', etc. are used loosely. The inhabitants' sense of community and identity must have changed constantly with time, but regional and smaller local divisions persisted.

28 A detailed description of the Giant's Ring complex is found in Barrie Hartwell, 'Prehistoric ritual at Ballynahatty, County Down' in E. Murray and P. Logue (eds), *Battles, Boats & Bones: Archaeological Discoveries in Northern Ireland 198–2008* (Belfast: Northern Ireland Environment Agency 2010), pp. 22–8.

29 See Cunliffe, *Europe Between the Oceans*, op. cit., for an overview of this development.

30 Already in the Mesolithic period pierced pieces of amber were worn around the Baltic and jet or jet-like substances were also used as ornaments. A long-distance gift exchange network developed during the Neolithic, bringing these materials to distant places, and this activity became more intense during the Bronze Age. The main source of jet was Whitby on the Yorkshire coast. Amber came from the Baltic.

31 Giraldus Cambrensis observed that the Irish still depended on a primitive variety of sheep from which the wool was pulled as they moulted at the time of the Norman invasion. This ancient sheep variety must have been rapidly replaced by more modern breeds that required shearing as the plucking of wool from sheep is never mentioned again. The earlier 'Soay' variety only survived on remote St Kilda.

32 See R. Loveday, *Inscribed across the Landscape* (London: Tempus 2006); A. Barclay and J. Harding (eds), *Pathways and Ceremonies, The Cursus Monuments of Britain and Ireland* (Oxford: Oxbow Books 1999).

33 Metalworkers are often represented in myths and folk tales as misshapen. They frequently had to work with toxic substances.

34 Faience was first produced in Egypt and Mesopotamia *c.*5000 BC, but like bronze production it got no further west than Crete and eastern Europe until it appeared in the British Isles at the same time as bronze working. Analysis of British and Irish faience reveals that the glaze contains copper and tin. It seems that the technique came with the metalworkers. Copper gave a turquoise or bluish hue to the glaze but tin gave no additional quality. Probably these ingredients were believed to have magical or talismanic qualities and that faience beads, like amber and jet ones, held healing and protective properties. See *British Archaeology*, 70, May 2003.

35 See B. Cunliffe and J.T. Koch, *Celtic from the West: Alternative Perspectives from Archaeology, Genetics, Language and Literature* (Oxford: Oxbow Books 2010) for information about the implications of DNA research into human population origins.

36 There were fortified towns in southern Iberia and along the north-Mediterranean coastlines, making a chain of semi-urbanized settlements stretching back to the Middle East. Corrstown was the only town in the northern parts of the Atlantic Fringe, underlining the importance of north Antrim on this Fringe route.

37 Many of the objects of personal finery, such as amber, faience or jet, had mystical qualities for their owners.

38 The *Duanaire Finn* is a manuscript compilation of late-medieval Fenian verse. It was written down by two scribes in the Spanish Netherlands in 1626–7 at the behest of Captain Somhairle Mac Domhnaill, from manuscripts belonging to other Irish exiles who were living there. The manuscript is now in the Franciscan Library, Dublin. See Eóin MacNeill and Gerard Murphy (ed. and transl.), *Duanaire Finn*, vols I, II and III (The Irish Texts Society, Dublin 1908, 1933 and 1953).

39 See Victoria Ginn and Stuart Rathbone, *Corrstown: A Coastal Community. Excavations of a Bronze Age Village in Northern Ireland* (Oxford: Oxbow Books 2012).

40 See Brian Smith and Alan Walker, *Rock Art and Ritual, Mindscapes of Prehistory* (Stroud: Amberley Publishing 2011).

41 Dáithí Ó hÓgáin, *The Lore of Ireland: An Encyclopedia of Myth, Legend and Romance* (Cork: The Collins Press 2006); Baillie and McCafferty, *The Celtic Gods*, op cit.

42 The level of destruction in the Middle East was enormous. Forty-seven major sites in Greece, Anatolia and the Near East (virtually all the known major sites of the period) were destroyed or burnt *c.*1225–1150 BC. This places the 1159 BC event neatly within its range. A comet or asteroid passing close to the earth could have sparked off earthquakes or caused fires as well as affecting the climate.

43 The hole contains small pieces of quartz that could have kept its penis in place.

44 The origins of the Indo-European languages and the development of the Celtic tongues are highly contentious issues. Colin Renfrew proposed in *Archaeology and Language* (London: Jonathan Cape 1987) that the Proto-Indo-European language was spoken by early farming communities in Anatolia. It then spread across Eurasia as the language of the Neolithic settlers and their communities. Amongst other opponents of this idea, David Anthony in *The Horse, The Wheel and Language: How Bronze-Age Riders from the Eurasian Steppes Shaped the Modern World* (Princeton and Oxford: Princeton University Press 2007) suggests that the Indo-European language originated amongst the herders on the Pontic Steppes, but the weight of archaeological, linguistic and DNA evidence supports Renfrew's theory. The DNA evidence indicates

that Europeans descend almost entirely from Anatolian stock in the male line, but largely from local hunter-gatherers in the female line. This suggests that young men would set out from an established Neolithic community to found a new one but that only a few women came with them, and so most women in the new community tended to be of local hunter-gatherer stock. Even so, the males' tongue, the language of Neolithic culture, was imposed on the community.

See Balaresque et al., 'A Predominantly Neolithic Origin'; P. Forster and C. Renfrew, 'Mother Tongue and Y Chromosomes', *Science* (9 September 2011); Colin Renfrew, *Archaeology and Language* (London: Jonathan Cape 1987); and P. Bellwood and C. Renfrew (eds), *Examining the Farming/Language Dispersal Hypothesis* (Cambridge: McDonald Institute 2003). Presumably the words relating to novel aspects of the Steppes pastoralist culture spread out across Eurasia with these innovations. Even the unrelated Basque language uses a form of the Indo-European word for a wheel. For the origins of the Celtic languages, see Barry Cunliffe and John Koch, *Celtic from the West: Alternative Perspectives from Archaeology, Genetics, Language and Literature* (Oxford: Oxbow Books 2010).

45 From *Topographia Hibernica* (*Topography of Ireland*), an account of the landscape and people of Ireland written by Gerald of Wales around 1188, soon after the Norman invasion of Ireland. It was the most influential work on Ireland in the Middle Ages.

46 See N. Campion, *The Dawn of Astrology: A Cultural History of Western Astrology, Volume I: The Ancient and Classical Worlds* (London: Continuum Books 2008) and N. Ostler, *Empires of the Word: A Language History of the World* (New York: Harper Perrenial 2005).

47 This is the only indication that horned helmets were used in Ireland.

48 The use of a faience bead in a gold pendant shows that these were high-status objects.

49 Baillie and McCafferty, *The Celtic Gods*, op. cit.

50 In Lisnacrogher, the peat cutters found 4 iron swords; 4 sword scabbards; 3 sword chapes and 2 possible chape fragments; 2 iron spearheads; and 19 spear butts with 17 spear shaft fragments. There were also 4 mounts; 2 ring-headed pins; a ribbon torc; a bronze necklet; 2 bronze bracelets; 2 spiral rings; 4 penannular rings; a stone bead; a bronze bowl; an iron axehead; adze head; sickle and billhook; as well as 8 decorated bronze mounts; 11 rings and 2 bronze strips.

51 Charles W. Jones (ed.), *From Medieval Literature in Translation* (London: Longman 1950).

52 From M. Dillon, *Tochmarc Étaíne in Irish Sagas* (Dublin: Early Irish Society 1959).

53 From Lucan, *Pharsalia III*. The *Pharsalia* is a great epic poem about Julius Caesar and his struggle with his various opponents.

54 It is also argued that he may have come from the southwest of Britain where a sub-Roman society survived for a long time. However, a strong case can be made for Birdoswald. A sub-Roman society continued in the north for a period. Patrick says that his family lived near a small town called Bannaven Taberniae, and Birdoswald fits well. An altar found there in 1821 was dedicated by the 'venatores Bannenses', 'the hunters of Banna', thus giving us the name of this settlement. Patrick's statement about his place of birth could read, 'vicus Banna venta Berniae', referring to 'the township of Banna'. See Charles Thomas, *Christianity in Roman Britain* (London: Thames & Hudson 1981), pp. 310–14; and Charles Thomas, *Celtic Britain* (London: Thames & Hudson 1986), pp. 123–8.

55 See D. Ó Cróinín (ed.), *A New History of Ireland. Volume I, Prehistoric and Early Ireland* (Oxford: OUP 2005), Chapter VII; D. Ó Cróinín, *A New History of Ireland 400–800* (Oxford: OUP 2005), pp. 182–233.

56 The term 'sept' here refers to a political or social entity based upon a family or clan.

57 See B. Wright, *Brigid: Goddess, Druidess and Saint* (Stroud: The History Press 2009).

58 From *De Excidio et Conquesto Britanniae* by Gildas (500–70), the most reliable British source for this period.

59 From G. Murphy, *Early Irish Lyrics Eighth to Twelfth Centuries* (Oxford: Clarendon Press 1977), translated by G. Murphy and Hector McDonnell.

60 Many early-Irish manuscripts are in the libraries of foreign foundations, as they were brought by Irish missionaries or written by them after they had settled abroad. Bobbio also has an early-Irish portable reliquary similar to the one illustrated.

61 The Altadeven St Patrick's Chair and 'well' is probably a pre-Christian ritual site. The story is told that St Patrick preached from the chair and baptized his converts with the *bullán*'s water. All the devils and serpents of Ireland dwelt here before St Patrick banished them into Lough Beag, the local lake. The festival of Lughnasa was observed here as 'Blaeberry Sunday' until the mid-twentieth century. See A. Rackard and L. O'Callaghan, *fishstonewater, holy wells of Ireland* (Cork: Atrium 2001).

62 See B. Freitag, *Sheela-Na-Gigs:Unravelling an Enigma* (London and New York: Routledge, Taylor & Francis Group 2004).

63 The *Landnámabók* (the Icelandic Book of Settlements, composed in the eleventh century) relates that the Norse found Irish priests in Iceland when they arrived, together with bells and crosiers. Irish accounts suggest that they only lived on Iceland during the summer months.

64 See H. McDonnell, *Margaret Stokes and the Irish Round Tower* (Belfast: UJA 1994); H. McDonnell, *Irish Round Towers* (Glastonbury: Wooden Books 2005).

65 See M. Stokes, *Early Christian Architecture in Ireland* (London: George Bell & Sons 1878).

66 No substantial buildings of Viking Dublin survive, even as foundations, but there were large stone and mortar houses and a cathedral as well as fortified walls and the wood and wattle buildings unearthed at Wood Quay.

67 Only the long northern side of the church and the tower at its western end remain. It most resembles contemporary continental Romanesque churches, which had symmetrical western facades with towers at each corner: see Hildesheim Cathedral (872 AD); St Cyriakus, Gernrode (961 AD); St Pantaleon, Cologne (966–80 AD). The church had a groin-vaulted interior.

68 Use of the stirrup depended upon solidly built saddles. The Irish also had no chain armour. They depended first upon the Vikings to provide fighting men in armour and later on the similarly equipped men from the Scottish Western Isles. Both groups also used broadswords and battle-axes.

69 These replaced the 'Soay'-type sheep the Irish had relied upon since Neolithic times.

70 Gallowglass is the anglicized form of *gallóglach* – a foreign fighter; the Hebrides were known as the Insi na nGall, the Foreigners' Islands. The crack native-Irish foot fighters were known as 'kerne'. They were lightly armed and would dash in and slash with their swords, throw their light javelins and then retire to rearm, while the gallowglass in their chain mail 'stood and fought'.

BIBLIOGRAPHY

Aldhouse-Green, M. and S., *The Quest for the Shaman: Shape-shifters, Sorcerers and Spirit Healers of Ancient Europe* (London: Thames & Hudson 2005).

Anthony, D., *The Horse, The Wheel and Language: How Bronze-Age Riders from the Eurasian Steppes Shaped the Modern World* (Princeton and Oxford: Princeton University Press 2007).

————— (ed.) with J.Y. Chi, *The Lost World of Old Europe: The Danube Valley, 5000–3500 BC* (Princeton and Oxford: The Institute for the Study of the Ancient World, New York University and Princeton University Press 2010).

Atroshenko, V.T. and Judith Collins, *The Origins of the Romanesque* (London: Lund Humphries 1985).

Bahn, P. and P. Pettitt, *Britain's Oldest Art: The Ice Age Cave Art of Creswell Crags* (London: English Heritage 2009).

Baillie, Michael, *A Slice Through Time: Dendrochronology and Precision Dating* (London: Routledge 1995).

—————, *Exodus to Arthur: Catastrophic Encounters with Comets* (London: Batsford Academic and Educational Ltd 1999).

—————, *The Celtic Gods: Comets in Irish Mythology* (Stroud: Tempus 2001).

————— and P. McCafferty, *The Celtic Gods: Comets in Irish Mythology* (Dundalk: Tempus, Dundalgan Press 2005).

Balaresque, P. et al., 'A Predominantly Neolithic Origin for European Paternal Lineages', *PLOS Biology* 8 (1), 2010.

Bannerman, J., *Studies in the History of Dalriada* (Edinburgh and London: Scottish Academic Press 1974).

Barclay, A. and Jan Harding (eds), *Pathways and Ceremonies: The cursus monuments of Britian and Ireland. Neolithic Studies Group Seminar Papers 4* (Oxford and Oakville: Oxbow Books 1999).

Bates, B., *The Real Middle-Earth: Magic and Mystery in the Dark Ages* (London: Sidgwick & Jackson 2003).

Bergh, S., *Landscape of the Monuments: A study of the passage tombs in the Cúil Irra region* (University of Stockholm: Riksantikvarieämbetet, Arkeologiska undersökningar, Skrifter nr 6 1995).

Bhreathnach, E. and C. Newman, *Tara* (Dublin: The Stationery Office 1995).

Bouckaert, Remco et al., 'Mapping the Origins and Expansion of the Indo-European Language Family', *Science*, 337, 6097 (2012), 957–60.

Bourke, C., *Patrick: The Archaeology of a Saint* (Belfast: HMSO 1993).

—————, *Studies in the Cult of Saint Columba* (Dublin: Four Courts Press 1997).

Bradley, R., *The Prehistory of Britain and Ireland* (Cambridge: Cambridge University Press 2007).

Burenhult, G. (ed.), *The Illustrated History of Humankind: People of the Stone Age, Hunter-gatherers and Early Farmers* (San Francisco: HarperCollins Publishers 1993).

Burl, A., *Prehistoric Astronomy and Ritual, Second Edition* (Colchester: Shire Archaeology 2005).

——, *The Stone Circles of the British Isles* (New Haven and London: Yale University Press 1976).

Campion, N., *The Dawn of Astrology: A Cultural History of Western Astrology, Volume 1: The Ancient and Classical Worlds* (London: Continuum Books 2008).

Carey, V., *Surviving the Tudors: The 'wizard' earl of Kildare and English rule in Ireland, 1537–1586* (Dublin: Four Courts Press 2002).

Chambers, A., *Granuaile: Grace O'Malley – Ireland's Pirate Queen c. 1530–1603* (Dublin: Gill & Macmillan 1979).

Cosgrove, A. (ed.), *A New History of Ireland: II Medieval Ireland 1169–1534* (Oxford: Oxford University Press 1987).

Cummings, V., *A View from the West: The Neolithic of the Irish Sea Zone* (Oxford: Oxbow Books 2009).

Cunliffe, B., *Europe Between the Oceans, Themes and Variations: 9000 BC–AD 1000* (New Haven and London: Yale University Press 2008).

—— and J.T. Koch, *Celtic from the West: Alternative Perspectives from Archaeology, Genetics, Language and Literature* (Oxford: Oxbow Books 2010).

Cunningham, B., *The World of Geoffrey Keating: History, myth and religion in seventeenth-century Ireland* (Dublin: Four Courts Press 2000).

Dark, K., *Britain and the End of the Roman Empire* (Letchworth: Tempus Press 2000).

De Paor, L. (transl.), *Saint Patrick's World: The Christian Culture of Ireland's Apostolic Age* (Dublin: Four Courts Press 1993).

Duffy, P., D. Edwards and E. FitzPatrick, *Gaelic Ireland c. 1250–1650: Land, Lordship and Settlement* (Dublin: Four Courts Press for the Group for the Study of Irish Historic Settlement 2001).

Duffy, S., *Robert the Bruce's Irish Wars: The Invasions of Ireland 1306–1329* (Letchworth: Tempus Press 2002).

Dumville, D., *Saint Patrick A.D. 493–1993* (Ipswich: The Boydell Press 1993).

Edwards, D., *Regions and Rulers in Ireland, 1100–1650: Essays for Kenneth Nicholls* (Dublin: Four Courts Press 2004).

Edwards, N., *The Archaeology of Early Medieval Ireland* (London: Batsford Academic and Educational Ltd 1990).

Eogan, G., *Knowth and the passage-tombs of Ireland* (London: Thames & Hudson 1986).

Evans, E.E., *Irish Heritage: The Landscape, The People and their Work* (Dundalk: W. Tempest Dundalgan Press 1967).

FitzPatrick, E., *Royal Inauguration in Gaelic Ireland c. 1100–1600: A Cultural Landscape* (Ipswich: The Boydell Press 2004).

Forster, P. and C. Renfrew, 'Mother Tongue and Y Chromosomes', *Science* (9 September 2011).

Freitag, B., *Sheela-Na-Gigs: Unravelling an enigma* (London and New York: Routledge, Taylor & Francis Group 2004).

Gimbutas, M., *The Languages of the Goddess* (San Francisco: HarperCollins Publishers 1991).

———, *The Living Goddesses* (Berkeley, Los Angeles and London: University of California Press 2001).

Hamlin, A. and C. Lynn (eds), *Pieces of the Past: Archaeological Excavations by the Department of the Environment for Northern Ireland 1970–1986* (Belfast: HMSO 1988).

Harbison, P., *Pre-Christian Ireland: From the First Settlers to the Early Celts* (London: Thames & Hudson 1988).

———, *Pilgrimage in Ireland: The Monuments and the People* (London: Barrie & Jenkins 1991).

Henry, F., *Irish Art in the Early Christian Period (to 800 A.D.)* (London: Methuen & Co. Ltd 1940).

———, *Irish Art during the Viking Invasions (800–1020 A.D.)* (London: Methuen & Co. Ltd 1967).

———, *Irish Art in the Romanesque Period (1020–1170 A.D.)* (London: Methuen & Co. Ltd 1970).

Herity, M. and G. Eogan, *Ireland in Prehistory* (London: Routledge & Kegan Paul 1977).

Hood, A.B.E. (ed. and transl.), *St. Patrick: His Writings and Muirchu's Life* (London: Phillimore & Co. Ltd 1978).

Howlett, D.R. (ed. and transl.), *The Book of Letters of Saint Patrick the Bishop* (Dublin: Four Courts Press 1994).

Hughes, K. and A. Hamlin, *Celtic Monasticism: The Modern Traveler to the Early Irish Church* (New York: The Seabury Press 1981).

Kinsella, T. (transl.), *The Táin* (London and New York: Oxford University Press 1970).

Laing, L., *The Archaeology of Late Celtic Britain and Ireland c. 400–1200 AD* (London: Methuen & Co. Ltd 1975).

Leask, H., *Irish Churches and Monastic Buildings, Volume One* (Dundalk: Dundalgan Press, W. Tempest Ltd 1955).

———, *Irish Churches and Monastic Buildings, Volume Two, Gothic Architecture to A.D. 1400* (Dundalk: Dundalgan Press, W. Tempest Ltd 1958).

———, *Irish Churches and Monastic Buildings, Volume Three, Medieval Gothic, The Last Phases* (Dundalk: Dundalgan Press, W. Tempest Ltd 1960).

Lewis-Williams, David, *The Mind in the Cave* (London: Thames & Hudson 2002).

——— and D. Pearce, *Inside the Neolithic Mind: Consciousness, Cosmos and the Realm of the Gods* (London: Thames & Hudson 2005).

Loveday, R., *Inscribed Across the Landscape: The Cursus Enigma* (Letchworth: Tempus 2006).

Leslie, S., *Saint Patrick's Purgatory: A Record from History and Literature* (London: Burns, Oates & Washbourne Ltd 1932).

Lynn, C., *Navan Fort Archaeology and Myth* (Belfast: Wordwell Ltd Ireland and Environment and Heritage Service 2003).

McCullough, D.W., *Wars of the Irish Kings: A Thousand Years of Struggle from the Age of Myth through the Reign of Queen Elizabeth I* (New York: Three Rivers Press 2002).

McDonnell, H., *Irish Round Towers* (Glastonbury: Wooden Books 2005).

McErlean, T. and N. Crothers, *Harnessing The Tides: The Early Medieval Tide Mills at Nendrum Monastery, Strangford Lough* (Belfast: The Stationery Office, Environment and Heritage Service 2007).

McMann, J., *Riddles of the Stone Age: Rock Carvings of Ancient Europe* (London: Thames & Hudson 1980).

McNamee, C., *The Wars of the Bruces: Scotland, England and Ireland 1306–1328* (Edinburgh: Tuckwell Press 1997).

MacNeill, M., *The Festival of Lughnasa: A Study of the Survival of the Celtic Festival of the Beginning of Harvest* (Oxford: Oxford University Press 1962).

McNeill, T.E., *Anglo-Norman Ulster: The History and Archaeology of an Irish Barony, 1177–1400* (Edinburgh: John Donald Publishers Ltd 1980).

Mallory, J.P., *In Search of the Indo-Europeans: Language, Archaeology and Myth* (London: Thames & Hudson 1991).

—— and T.E. McNeill, *The Archaeology of Ulster from Colonization to Plantation* (Belfast: The Institute of Irish Studies, Queen's University Belfast 1991).

Meehan, C., *The Traveller's Guide to Sacred Ireland: A Guide to the Sacred Places of Ireland, Her Legends, Folklore & People* (Glastonbury: Gothic Image Publications 2002).

Milburn, R., *Early Christian Art and Architecture* (London: Wildwood House 1988).

Mithen, S., *After the Ice: A Global Human History, 20,000–5000 BC* (London: Weidenfeld & Nicolson 2003).

Mohen, J., *The World of Megaliths* (London: Cassell Publishers Ltd 1989).

Molyneaux, T., *A Discourse concerning the Danish mounts, forts and towers in Ireland* in G. Boate (ed.), *A Natural History of Ireland* (London: 1725).

Morgan, H., *Tyrone's Rebellion: The Outbreak of the Nine Years War in Tudor Ireland* (Suffolk: The Boydell Press 1993).

Murphy, G., *Early Irish Lyrics Eighth to Twelfth Centuries* (Oxford: Clarendon Press 1977).

Murray, E. and P. Logue (eds), *Battles, Boats & Bones: Archaeological Discoveries in Northern Ireland 198–2008* (Belfast: Northern Ireland Environment Agency 2010).

Mytum, H., *The Origins of Early Christian Ireland* (London and New York: Routledge 1992).

Nur, Amos, *Apocalypse, Earthquakes, Archaeology and the Wrath of God* (Princeton and Oxford: Princeton University Press 2008).

O'Brien, W., *Bronze Age Copper Mining in Britain and Ireland* (Colchester: Shire Archaeology 1996).

Ó Cróinín, D. (ed.), *A New History of Ireland: Prehistoric and Early Ireland* (Oxford: OUP 2005).

——, *Longman History of Ireland: Early Medieval Ireland 400–1200* (London and New York: Longman 1995).

Ó Floinn, R., *Irish Shrines & Reliquaries of the Middle Ages* (Country House and The National Museum of Ireland 1994).

Ó hÓgáin, Dáithí, *The Lore of Ireland: An Encyclopedia of Myth, Legend and Romance* (Cork: The Collins Press 2006).

O'Kelly, Michael, *Newgrange, Archaeology, Art and Legend* (London: Thames & Hudson 2004).

O'Rahilly, T.F., *Early Irish History and Mythology* (Dublin 1946).

Osgood, R. and S. Monks, with J. Toms, *Bronze Age Warfare* (Stroud: The History Press 2000).

Ostler, N., *Empires of the Word: A Language History of the World* (New York and London: Harper Perennial 2005).

O'Sullivan, M., *Dún na nGall: The Mound of the Hostages, Tara* (Dublin: Wordwell Ltd and UCD, School of Archaeology 2005).

Perlès, C., *The Early Neolithic in Greece: The first farming communities in Europe* (Cambridge: Cambridge University Press 2001).

Picard, J., *Ireland and Northern France AD 600–850* (Dublin: Four Courts Press 1991).

Potter, T.W. and C. Johns, *Roman Britain* (London: The British Museum Press 1992).

Rackard, A. and L. O'Callaghan, *fishstonewater: holy wells of Ireland* (Cork: Atrium 2001).

Raftery, B., *Pagan Celtic Ireland: The Enigma of the Irish Iron Age* (London: Thames & Hudson 1994).

Renfrew, Colin, *Archaeology and Language* (London: Jonathan Cape 1987).

——— and P. Bellwood (eds), *Examining the Farming/Language Dispersal Hypothesis* (Cambridge: McDonald Institute 2003).

Richardson, H. and J. Scarry, *An Introduction to Irish High Crosses* (Dublin: Mercier Press 1990).

Rudgley, R., *Lost Civilisations of the Stone Age* (London: Century 1998).

———, *The Alchemy of Culture: Intoxicants in Society* (London: British Museum Press 1993).

Scarre, C., *The Megalithic Monuments of Britain & Ireland* (London: Thames & Hudson 2007).

———, *Landscapes of Neolithic Brittany* (Oxford: Oxford University Press 2012).

Smith, Brian and Alan Walker, *Rock Art and Ritual, Mindscapes of Prehistory* (Stroud: Amberley Publishing 2011).

Stokes, M., *Early Christian Architecture in Ireland* (London: George Bell and Sons 1878).

Stout, G., *Newgrange and the Bend of the Boyne* (Cork: Cork University Press 2002).

Thom, A., *Megalithic Lunar Observatories* (Oxford: Clarendon Press 1971).

———, *Megalithic Sites in Britain* (Oxford: Clarendon Press 1967).

Thomas, C., *Christianity in Roman Britain to AD 500* (London: Batsford Academic and Educational Ltd 1981).

———, *Celtic Britain* (London: Thames & Hudson 1986).

Waddell, J., J. Fenwick and K. Barton, *Rathcroghan: Archaeological and geophysical survey in a ritual landscape* (Dublin: Wordwell Ltd 2009).

Waterman, D.M., *Excavations at Navan Fort 1961–71: Northern Ireland Monographs: No. 3* (Belfast: The Stationery Office 1997).

Welsh, H., *Tomb Travel: A Guide to Northern Ireland's megalithic monuments* (Belfast: Northern Ireland Environment Agency 2011).

Wright, B., *Brigid: Goddess, Druidess and Saint* (Stroud: The History Press 2009).

INDEX